Listening for God

Volume 2

CONTEMPORARY LITERATURE
AND THE LIFE OF FAITH

Listening FOR God

Volume 2

Contributing

Editors

Paula J. Carlson

Peter S. Hawkins

Augsburg Fortress
Minneapolis

813.54
Carlson

LISTENING FOR GOD, Volume 2
Contemporary Literature and the Life of Faith

This Reader is accompanied by a Leader Guide and a Videocassette.

Developed in cooperation with the Institute of Sacred Music, Worship and the Arts, Yale University, New Haven, Connecticut.

Production made possible in part by a grant from the Lilly Endowment Inc., Indianapolis, Indiana.

Cover painting: "Sunrise Pond" by James Wilcox Dimmers / photo by Ann DeLaVergne. Copyright © James Wilcox Dimmers. Used by permission.

Cover design: Koechel Peterson & Associates Inc.

Editors: Mary Nasby Lohre and Carolyn F. Lystig

The Library of Congress has cataloged volume one as follows:
Listening for God : contemporary literature and the life of faith/
   contributing editors, Paula J. Carlson, Peter S. Hawkins
        p.   cm
    ISBN 0-8066-2715-8
      1. American literature—Christian authors. 2. Christian life—
Literary collections. 3. American literature—20th century.
4. Faith—Literary collections.   I. Carlson, Paula J.   II. Hawkins, Peter S.
PS508.C54L57 1994
813'.54080382—dc20
                                      96-50662
                                         CIP

Manufactured in the U.S.A.   ISBN 0-8066-2844-8   AF 10-28448

00   99   5   6   7   8   9   10

Contents

Acknowledgments

"Short Easter" from *The Afterlife and Other Stories* by John Updike. Copyright © 1994 by John Updike. Reprinted by permission of Alfred A. Knopf, Inc. and The Penguin Group.

"People Who Don't Know the Answers" from *Saint Maybe* by Anne Tyler. Copyright © 1991 by ATM, Inc. Reprinted by permission of Alfred A. Knopf, Inc. and A. M. Heath & Company, Ltd.

"Saved" from *Colored People* by Henry Louis Gates, Jr. Copyright © 1994 by Henry Louis Gates, Jr. Reprinted by permission of Alfred A. Knopf, Inc. and The Penguin Group.

"The Rich Brother" from *Back in the World* by Tobias Wolff. Copyright © 1981 by Tobias Wolff. Reprinted by permission of International Creative Management, Inc.

"After the Baptism" from *The Tomcat's Wife* by Carol Bly. Copyright © 1991 by Carol Bly. Reprinted by permission of HarperCollins Publishers, Inc.

"An Intermediate Stop" from *Dream Children* by Gail Godwin. Copyright © 1976 by Gail Godwin. Reprinted by permission of Alfred A. Knopf, Inc. and John Hawkins & Associates, Inc.

"Seeing," "Weather Report: August 9," and "Getting to Hope" from *Dakota*. Copyright © 1993 by Kathleen Norris. Reprinted by permission of Ticknor & Fields/Houghton Mifflin Co. All rights reserved.

"A Father's Story" from *The Times Are Never So Bad* by Andre Dubus. Copyright © 1983 by Andre Dubus. Reprinted by permission of David R. Godine, Publisher, Inc.

Introduction

In her essay "Teaching a Stone to Talk" the writer Annie Dillard describes listening for God. You begin to listen, she says, by declaring: "Now I am ready. Now I will stop and be wholly attentive. You empty yourself and wait, listening."[1]

The selections in *Listening for God, Volume 2* offer new opportunities to listen closely, to hear the ways that eight contemporary American writers address religious issues and present religious people. The authors included here write their stories and essays from a variety of perspectives. They may, like Annie Dillard, have committed their "life's length to listening"[2] for God; they may be less forthright about their listening; or perhaps they may be wary of such an endeavor. But in the work of all these authors we will hear contemporary conversation about religion, and we will hear how some influential writers present or respond to religious people's commitment to listen for God.

The writers included in the *Listening for God* resources are all important American writers born between 1925 and 1950. They have all earned the American literary culture's marks of success. Their books are published by major publishing houses and are reviewed in the most influential periodicals. Most of these authors have won notable awards: Pulitzer prizes, National Book Awards, PEN/Faulkner prizes, and others as well.

These writers' audiences, however, are not limited to prize committees or academic circles. Some of the authors have written best sellers. Some regularly present their work on television or radio programs. Some write for popular magazines or newspapers. Some have had their work made into films. The audiences these writers speak to are diverse and large. The explorations of religious questions that appear in their work, then, take place in a large context, one centered in mainstream American literary culture but reaching beyond that as well.

The conversations stimulated by these writers may take many courses. The writers speak from various religious traditions. From this second volume of *Listening for God,* Andre Dubus and Tobias Wolff are Roman Catholics; Gail Godwin and Henry Louis Gates, Jr., are Episcopalians; John

Updike grew up a Lutheran and has attended Congregational and Episcopal churches; Kathleen Norris is a member of a Presbyterian church and also a Benedictine oblate; Carol Bly has attended Lutheran and Episcopal churches; and Anne Tyler's parents are Quakers. The writers have been shaped, then, by a variety of Christian traditions. Some now speak with varying degrees of openness about their religious beliefs, while others, such as Anne Tyler, prefer not to speak about those beliefs at all. And while some of these writers—Norris, Dubus, Godwin, and Updike—now place themselves firmly within particular churches, others—Bly and Tyler, for instance—are explorers of religious issues but remain outside traditional churches.

Mirroring the diversity in perspective of the eight writers in this volume is a diversity in approach to religious issues. For some of them, such as Bly and Norris, religion is a frequent topic. For others, such as Tyler, Gates, and Godwin, it is a rarer one. None of these authors, though, is known primarily as a "religious" writer. The writers whose works are included in this volume approach religion as one among many topics. They explore it in the context of other concerns.

What might we hear, then, when we listen to the array of conversations about God that the stories and essays in this volume contain and stimulate? Most importantly, we will hear the questions of people—authors or their characters—who directly face the religious nature of their experiences. We will hear some possible responses to these questions, but we will also encounter uncertainty, and we may find ourselves unwilling to accept either the answers or the ambiguity in the stories. Our responses to the conversations *within* the stories, then, may feed our conversations *about* the stories. Immersed in this interplay of conversation, we may raise our own questions and speak from our own traditions about the mystery of listening for God.

Paula J. Carlson

Notes

1. Annie Dillard, *Teaching a Stone to Talk* (New York: Harper & Row, 1982), 72.
2. *Teaching a Stone to Talk*, 72.

1

John Updike

John Updike is among the most prolific of American authors: to date there are sixteen published novels, a *Collected Poems* that brings together the work of four decades, five volumes of essays and criticism, and now, with the 1994 publication of *The Afterlife*, eleven collections of short stories. Updike has come to be known for the extraordinary richness of his prose as well as for its sheer abundance. More particularly, he has become famous as a chronicler of married life (and its failures) within the confines of small-town Pennsylvania or among the white Anglo-Saxon Protestant upper-middle classes of Boston and New York. Along with considerable acclaim, however, has come notoriety: Updike's vivid, indeed graphic, portrayals of sexuality—and more specifically, of sexual adultery—have turned away some readers and brought on the censure of critics impatient with what they dismiss as adolescent obsessions.

What is too often lost in discussion of Updike's work, however, is the degree to which he is driven by theology. His self-identification as a Christian is made explicit in his 1989 memoir, *Self-Consciousness*, where he describes his Lutheran religious upbringing and present churchgoing, the importance of such writers as Soren Kierkegaard and Karl Barth to his intellectual formation, and his own sense of God as "a dark sphere enclosing the pinpoint of our selves, an adamant bubble enclosing us, protecting us, enabling us to let go, to ride the waves of what is."[1]

But one does not need Updike's nonfiction to reveal these convictions and allegiances. There is the greater witness of his fiction itself, as seen in the explicit theologizing of an early story like "Pigeon Feathers," in the tortured clergyman protagonists of such novels as *A Month of Sundays* (1975) or *Roger's Version* (1986), and in the sustained look at American life stretching between 1960 and 1990 in the four *Rabbit* novels. Recognizing in all of his work the irresistible "itch of theology," Cynthia Ozick even goes as far as to say, "Updike is our chief Dante: America is his heaven and hell."[2]

If Updike is, in fact, the poet of our late twentieth-century *Divine Comedy*, explorer of our secularized "afterlife," his theological vision is shaped more by Kierkegaard and Barth than by any other spiritual mentors. Like them, he rejects liberal, humanistic Protestantism. He has often quoted with approval Barth's remark that "one cannot speak of God by speaking of man in a loud voice"[3] and emphasized the great gulf fixed between ourselves and the divine, an abyss that only God is able to bridge. His characters will do almost anything to avoid this crossing: like Rabbit Angstrom, they have "no taste for the dark, tangled, visceral aspect of Christianity, the *going through* quality of it, the passage *into* death and suffering that redeems and inverts these things."[4] And yet what Updike's fiction does, in effect, is eliminate any other authentic way "through" existence, leaving the reader instead with a purely secular life exposed as a dead end: "Sex or death, you pick your poison."[5]

The author's vocation, then, is to tell the truth about us as he sees it: to describe moral dilemmas and adulteries of all kinds; to show human problems that have no human solutions; to depict the "erosions and betrayals" that, along with death itself, are all a sign of our fallen condition. "What small faith I have has given me what artistic courage I have. My theory was that God already knows everything and cannot be shocked. And only truth is useful. Only truth can be built on."[6]

Unlike so much of his other work, the short stories gathered in *The After-life* are not overtly theological. Its characters do not listen for God; instead, they attend to irregularities in their own heartbeat, paying attention to receding gums and hairlines. All of them are growing old if not actually growing up. The call of the past is always powerful, as they look back with longing and regret on sex, careers, childhood homes, old lovers, and the lost battles of first marriages. On the other hand, what they look forward to—with different measures of panic and denial—is death.

In the collection's title story, for instance, the Billingses visit their former best friends in England and discover that the couple's decision to take an early retirement has enabled them to fulfill a dream of country living far away from "the vulgarity, the beggary, the violence" of America. In many ways the Egglestons have made their Anglophile fantasy come true—filling days with horse riding and gardening, forays in quest of affordable antiques, and the doing of good works in the local village. Nonetheless, the story is pervaded by a sense of uneasiness, especially on the part of Carter Billings.

On the first night of the visit, what could very well have been a lethal fall down a darkened staircase gradually becomes a kind of "wake up call" to the fact of his own mortality. England is meant to be a refuge from violence; but even there it is apparent that life is fragile, as winds from the North Sea threaten destruction and ancient tree limbs succumb to the rages of a storm. But as well as the foreshadowing of doom, the story is also shot through with the intimation of angels—harbingers of the "afterlife"?—whose presence is caught in the sudden glimpse of a heron's six-foot wingspread or in the latticework of electrical power lines seen as if marching in procession, "with a ghostly delicacy against the black sky."[7] Without telling the reader *what* to make of this real or imagined flutter, the story asks us to come to terms with it, perhaps even to court rather than run away from these mysterious "angels."

In "The Journey to the Dead," however, it is the instinct to run away that takes over. Reunited by chance with Arlene Quint, an old college friend, Martin Fredericks finds himself pleasurably revisiting the past through the eyes of someone who was with him in the old days, "those Fifties and early Sixties when you moved toward your life with an unstressed freedom no one could understand, now, who had not been young then."[8] Times have changed, however, and Arlene's cancer forces her to confront the mortality that his good health enables him to sidestep. Visiting her hospital room after a stroke and shortly before her death, Fredericks is overcome by a desire to be elsewhere.

He recalls the epic literature studied long ago in college—*Gilgamesh*, the *Odyssey*, the *Aeneid*—where living heroes flee from their encounters with the underworld in a desperate bid to escape the inevitable. Robbed of her voice by the stroke, Arlene greets all attempts at bedside humor with an unsmiling stare, as if to acknowledge Fredericks's unspoken perception that "the dead hate us, and we hate the dead." Then, promising insincerely to visit again, he, "like the heroes before him, fled." The story seems to bear out T. S. Eliot's assertion in the *Four Quartets* that "human kind / Cannot bear very much reality."[9]

Running away is less easy to pull off in "Short Easter." Fogel is a man financially well off, with an enviable amount of worldly security, who also feels himself past his prime. He finds that on the highway other cars seem frequently to tailgate his Mercedes, as if he were falling behind—losing time rather than making it. This sense of loss is made explicit by having the story take place on a particular Easter Sunday when Daylight Savings makes time "spring forward" and, thereby, steal an hour: "Because the clocks had been jumped ahead, the day kept feeling in retard of where it actually was. It was later than he thought" *(Reader, 18)*. Even Fogel's house seems to participate in this entropy, as its creaks, decay, and "irreversible expenditures of energy" mirror his personal sense of running down.

We're told from the outset that for Fogel, Easter itself had always been a holiday "without punch," an occasion of disappointing egg hunts and boozy champagne brunches, perhaps most memorable as the anniversary of the end of a love affair decades earlier—a reminder not of Resurrection but that "all things end" *(Reader, 15)*. Nonetheless, he is miffed when his wife proposes a morning of yard work rather than entertaining the possibility that he might want to go to church, even if only for the sake of nostalgia. Christianity has no deep hold over his life, and yet (unlike his wife) the fact that the day is Easter means something to him—something he can neither name nor get out of his mind.

When at the end of the story he wakes from an afternoon nap in blank fear, he realizes that, although everything in his world seems to be in place, "yet something was immensely missing" *(Reader, 20)*. Such a revelation is a far cry from the disciples' Easter discovery. Nonetheless, it represents for Fogel a genuine moment of truth. Nothing he possesses can make up for what he lacks, nor can anything in his comfortable suburban world fill the immense need for something more.

Peter S. Hawkins

Notes

1. John Updike, *Self-Consciousness: Memoirs* (New York: Alfred A. Knopf, 1989), 229.

2. Cynthia Ozick, *Art & Ardor* (New York: Alfred Knopf, 1983), 122.

3. Bernard A. Schopen, "Faith, Morality, and the Novels of John Updike," *Critical Essays on John Updike*, ed. William R. Macnaughton (Boston: G. K. Hall, 1982), 196.

4. John Updike, *Rabbit, Run* (New York: Alfred A. Knopf, 1960), 237.

5. "Playing with Dynamite," *The Afterlife and Other Stories* (New York: Alfred A. Knopf, 1994), 262.

6. *Self-Consciousness*, 231.

7. "The Afterlife," *The Afterlife*, 18.

8. "The Journey to the Dead," *The Afterlife*, 68.

9. T. S. Eliot, "Burnt Norton," *T. S. Eliot: The Complete Poems and Plays, 1909–1950* (New York: Harcourt, Brace and Company, 1962), 118.

Short Easter

Fogel could not remember its ever happening before—the advent of Daylight Saving Time clipping an hour off Easter. Church bells rang in the dark; the pious would be scrambling about in their topcoats and hats turning the clocks ahead. All day, the reluctantly budding earth would wear its crown of cloudy firmament a bit awry. Easter had always struck Fogel as a holiday without real punch, though there was, among the more vivid of his childhood memories, a magical peep into a big sugar egg; it had been at his aunt's house, in Connecticut, where the houses seemed cleaner than in New Jersey, the people wealthier, the daffodils a brighter yellow. Inside the egg, paper silhouettes spelled out a kind of landscape—a thatch-roofed cottage, a rabbit wearing a vest, a fringe of purple flowers, a receding path and paper mountains—all bathed in an unexpectedly brilliant light. Where had the light come from? There must have been a hole in the egg besides the one he peeped into, a kind of skylight, admitting to this miniature world a celestial illumination.

But, generally, the festivity that should attend the day had fallen rather flat: quarrelsome and embarrassed family church attendances, with nobody quite comfortable in pristine Easter clothes; melancholy egg hunts in some muddy back yard, the smallest child confused and victimized; headachy brunches where the champagne punch tasted sour and conversation lagged. Perhaps if Fogel had not been led to live north of Boston, where at Eastertide croci and daffodils poked up through dead lawns like consciously brave thoughts and even forsythia was shy of blooming, nature might have encouraged the ostensible mood of hope and beginning again. But the day was usually raw, and today was no exception—a day of drizzle and chill, only an hour less of it.

Fogel was sixty-two, and felt retirement drawing closer. In the daily rub he discovered all sorts of fresh reasons for irritation. The line at the post office was held up by people buying money orders, and the line at the grocery store by people buying state lottery tickets. It seemed to him sheer willful obstructionism. Why didn't these people have checking accounts, and do their gambling on the stock market, as he did? Driving to work, on those

days when he did not take the commuter train, Fogel resented being tailgated, and especially by young drivers, and very especially by young men in
sunglasses, their identity further shielded by tinted windshields and newly
fashionable opaque side windows. One morning, the car behind him, a low
scarlet sports model, wore a kind of mask or muzzle of dark vinyl over its
grille, and this ultra-chic, ultra-protective touch infuriated him, just as did
cardboard sunshields in parked cars, and leather-ridged, fingertipless driving gloves, and fuzz-busters blatantly fastened above dashboards, and
bumper stickers declaring SHIT HAPPENS or ironically commanding SUPPORT
WILDLIFE—THROW A PARTY. The vinyl-faced car was frantic to pass, and
nosed toward the right and, finding there an onrolling eighteen-wheeler,
nosed back and swerved left, into a lane that in a few hundred yards termi-
nated in a blinking yellow arrow. Fogel pressed on the accelerator, to keep
abreast of the boy and hold him out in the doomed lane. Fogel smiled behind
the wheel, picturing the other car's satisfying crash into the great arrow—
the raucous grating of metal, the misty explosion of glass, and himself sail-
ing serenely on in his middle lane. But the boy, getting the picture, cut in so
sharply that Fogel had to brake or hit him; he chose to hit the brakes, and
the youthful driver, steering one-handed, held up the middle finger of the
other hand for Fogel to see as the red car, belching, pulled away.

If Fogel's stately Mercedes had been equipped with a button that annihi-
lated other vehicles, he would have used it three or four times a mile. Almost
every other automobile on the road—those that passed him, those so slow
he had to pass them, those going just his speed and hanging in his side mir-
rors like pursuing furies—seemed a deliberate affront, restricting his freedom and being somehow *pretentious* about it. What was the point of that
sinister Darth Vader–like mask over a grille? No point, just pure intimida-
tion. Which was, he had come through sixty years to realize, the aim of
eighty-five percent of all human behavior.

His body's accumulating failures also angered him. His eyelashes kept
falling into his eyes, and the presbyopia of late middle age prevented him
from seeing, in the mirror, his own eyes well enough to take the lashes out.
A tantalizing refusal of focus, like the pressure of water that keeps us from
seizing a tempting shell on the sandy bottom of six feet of crystalline sea,
frustrated him, and when he put on his reading glasses he could see the dark
curved foreign body but not get his fingers and the corner of a handkerchief
in behind the lenses to remove it. So he would blink and grimace and curse
and wish he had a young wife; his wife's vision was no better than his own,
and dismissingly she said things like "It will work its way out" or "Maybe it
just *feels* like an eyelash." His mother, he could not help but remember,

would deftly stab away with a folded piece of toilet paper a fleck of dirt that was tormenting his sensitive cornea. But his mother, he realized now, at the time had been half his present age, though she had seemed ageless, enormous, and omnipotent.

Flying back from New York to Boston late one afternoon this past winter, he had sat across the aisle from a young man and woman, both about thirty, who evidently had not known each other before taking seats side by side. The man was a bit beefy, with a reddish-blond mustache and thinning pale hair; the woman, all but eclipsed from Fogel's angle, held a large cardboard folder and seemed to be in a state of some excitement. Her hands, gesturing and flickering in front of the oval airplane window, appeared ringless and agitated. Her voice, as she explained herself—the advertising agency she was taking the folder to, her mixed feelings about living in New York, her roommate's sayings and comical attitude toward life—did a penetrating dance, tireless and insistent, though her voice was high and light. Perhaps she was less than thirty—just starting out, testing her powers. She talked incessantly but, as it were, abashedly, throwing her words out in a feathery way, as if to soften their impact. "Yeahhh?" she would add, nonsensically, to a sentence, and she put on a soft quick giggle, a captivating titter, a kind of shimmer of shyness in which she wrapped her unrelenting verbal assault upon her seatmate, who responded—how could he not?—with ever more murmurous and authoritative replies, concerning cities and work and all other areas where he might be supposed to wield male expertise. This man's chunky pale hands began to gesture, to chop the air; he pompously crossed and recrossed his legs and preeningly lifted his shoe, rotating the tip; his voice grew gravelly and confiding as the feathery, questioning, giggling, excited voice of the other assaulted his ear and, unintentionally, Fogel's.

Fogel had been talked to, in the course of his life, by a woman in a voice exactly like this. It had been a bath, her voice, in which he grew weightless, an iridescent bubbly uplifting in which floated always a question, the lilting teasing female question, to which his maleness, clumsy and slow to comprehend though it was, was the only answer. He and this woman, Fogel further remembered, had come, twenty-some years ago, to an unhappy end, which had seemed tragic and hard to swallow at the time but which now, to this elderly man sitting above the clouds while the engines droned and the stewardesses struggled to distribute drinks and the girl across the aisle deliciously prattled and her naked hands flickered against the deepening darkness of the airplane window, appeared merely inevitable, since all things end. One small side effect still rankled: their affair ended in the springtime, and his former mistress declined to invite him and his family to an Easter-egg hunt she and her husband annually gave. His children's feelings were hurt, and for consolation they were taken out, after church, to eat at the local International House of Pancakes. Heaps of pancakes, Fogel remembered—buckwheat, buttermilk, blueberry—that seemed, soaked in syrup, almost unswallowably sweet.

And yet, when the plane landed and the scramble to retrieve things from the overhead rack took over, Fogel forgot to look, as he had been intending, at the young woman, to check out her height, her hips, her face full on, her lovely long lively hands, to see if they were truly ringless. While his attention was elsewhere or nowhere she must have stood and brushed her backside past his and out of his life forever. She remained with him only as a voice, the perennial voice of flirtation.

Fogel's absent-mindedness was becoming alarming. On this strangely short Easter, as bells prodded the air in the town below the hill where he lived, he walked to his mailbox to retrieve the morning *Globe,* and his old gray-muzzled dog, a Labrador retriever, flushed the six or so mourning doves that gathered on a warm open slope, amid scrub brush, above the curving driveway. Every weekend morning, Saturday and Sunday, this happened, the dog ponderously charging forward and the mourning doves thrashing into the air with an abrupt whistle and merged beating of wings, and yet Fogel always forgot it would happen and was startled, so that his heart raced, his blood leaping like another dove. His heart would keep thumping as he walked back up the hill with the many-sectioned, pretentious, intimidating Sunday newspaper in his arms. The thumping felt dangerous, and he felt endangered when his wife, at breakfast, proposed that he help her with the spring raking. "We were unforgivably sloppy last fall," she said. "We left leaves under all the bushes and over by the rocks, and now they'll smother the new growth if we don't dig them out." She was a native of these Northern parts, and knew the ways of its weather. "You can't trust the lawn boys to do it; it was their stupid useless blower that put the leaves there in the first place. They didn't have these leaf-blowers when I was a girl; my father's gardeners *raked.*"

Unlike those of the girl on the plane, this woman's powers were long established, and she felt no need to test them. She moved back and forth between kitchen island and sink, between sink and refrigerator and stove, with an insatiable silver-haired energy. As Fogel sat at the breakfast table with the newspaper, trying to remember which sections he had already read, he felt pushed from behind, tailgated. How did she know he hadn't, sentimentally, decided to go to church? "I'll never forget," she went on, "the year we went to Morocco and didn't get the leaves off the front beds until May and the poor tulips had all grown *inches* under the mulch—horrible, these pathetic white snaky stems growing sideways! Once the sun got to them they straightened up but all summer until they died back were shaped like the letter L. They all had elbows!" This monologue, he recognized, was a matured version, hardened into jagged edges and points that prodded and hurt, of the young woman's feathery, immersing discourse across the airplane aisle—a version of that female insistence upon getting male attention, a force as irresistible as the ability of freezing water to split rocks.

"I'm trying to read the paper," Fogel pointed out.

"I think it's grotesque, it's absolutely *dodd*ery," she said, "the way you've taken to dawdling over the paper, even the real-estate section, even the cooking tips. It's a bad habit you've gotten into from killing time on the train. Nobody expects you to read *everything*—they just want you to glance at the ads."

"Isn't it rather cold and dismal outdoors?" he asked.

"No more so than it ever is this time of year. The longer we work, the warmer it will get. If you think about it, darling, the sun this time of year is as strong as an August sun, though it doesn't feel that way. Don't be a doddery dawdler; come *on*—one hour of good stiff yard work and then the Allisons' brunch and you can watch the football playoffs."

"They're over."

"Are they honestly? I thought they were endless."

"You were confused by the Hula Bowl. It's hockey and basketball now."

"How can you tell? It's all just ugly brutes bashing into each other. It's horrible, the way television has turned violence into a joke." She had suddenly left the kitchen.

Meekly, draggingly, Fogel followed. Pulling moist compacted oak leaves from underneath the forsythia and lilacs, careful not to let a budding twig poke his eye, Fogel was reminded of an Easter-egg hunt, and in his reverie, while his wife swooped back and forth with sheets of last year's leaves and bundles of brisk directives, his brooding mind warmed his old indignation at not having been invited to that party given by his then recently forsaken inamorata. She could have trusted him. He would have stood off to one side and been distant and discreet while his children hunted and his wife mixed it up socially. Insult was added to injury when, some months later, at a third family's house, he was shown home movies of the day—the scampering children, their faces in close-up smeared with chocolate and anxiety at not getting their share; the men in business suits and pastel shirts, standing on the brown lawn in little conferences of three or four, holding wine glasses and pâté-laden crackers; and the women, all in mini-skirts in that era, swooping about after their children with brown paper bags and discarded sweaters. It was a familiar scene, year after year, except that this year he was not in it; no matter how the camera panned and skidded from group to group, Fogel was invisible. His former mistress wore a glistening purple dress, he seemed to remember, that just barely covered her bustling hindquarters, and she clowned for the camera when it came her way, her lips moving to frame a gay feathery voice that was inaudible.

How tenacious, really, forsythia is of last fall's leaves! And the English ivy was worse yet, more clingy and snaggy. The teeth of Fogel's little bamboo bush rake kept snapping in the struggle with hostile vegetation. One of his fantasies was a kind of ray gun that, directed at a plant or tree, would not only kill it but instantly vaporize it into a fine, fertilizing ash. Agricultural labor, this endless plucking of weeds and replowing of fields, had always seemed to him the essence of futility; after sixty years he was coming to realize that all work, legal or medical or, like his own, financial, was also a Sisyphean matter of recycling, of pushing inert and thankless matter back and forth, of turning over (in his case) the profoundly rich compost of corporate debt. All labor was tied to human life, life as pointless as that of any new little jade-green weed already joyously sprouting beneath the damp-blackened leaves.

The Allisons' brunch was also pointless—the same dozen aging couples, with three widows and a bachelor, that they saw every weekend. Throughout the gathering Fogel kept trying to glimpse, out of the corners of his eyes, the shoulders of his navy-blue blazer, and brushing at the white hairs that kept appearing there; he was shedding. To get himself through a strenuous conversation on the future of yachting after this winter's debacle in San Diego, he accepted a second Bloody Mary. Then he prudently switched to the faintly sour, platinum-colored champagne punch. One widow told him he should take his cholesterol count very seriously; if her husband had, she wouldn't be a widow now. Tears suddenly troubled her eyes, with their cobalt-blue contact lenses. Another woman, in a purplish dress, came up to Fogel and pressed her wrinkled face upward toward him as if straining to see through a besmirched skylight, and launched her voice into an insistent sweet sing-song. He regretted that no movie camera—a video camera was what they used now, with a built-in sound track—was at work recording the fact that he was here, at this party: that he had been invited. He and his wife left at two-thirty, which felt nearer noon than that. Because the clocks had been jumped ahead, the day kept feeling in retard of where it actually was. It was later than he thought. The cold drizzle intensified, and discouraged returning to the yard work; the bursitis in his shoulders ached from all that reaching with the rake. He found some golf on television. The tour had moved east from the desert events, with lavender mountains in the background and emerald fairways posed upon sand and cactus and with ancient

Hollywood comedians as tournament sponsors, to courses in the American South, with trees in tender first leaf and azaleas in lurid bloom. Young blond men putted, over and over, for birdies. A tremendous drowsiness seized Fogel as he watched within his easy chair. The fresh air and yard work, the gin and tomato juice, the champagne and the effort to be sociable all added up to a crushing accumulation.

Stealthily, avoiding his own bedroom, where his wife could be heard chattering on the telephone to one of her myriad of woman friends, he took a section of the newspaper that perhaps he had not already read and lay down on the bed in their younger son's old room. Posters of European cars and American rock stars were still on the walls, though the boy had left for college over ten years ago. His mother liked to keep the room as he had left it, as some fanatical religious sects keep a room ready in case Jesus returns and asks to be a guest. A pipe rattled—fresh steam hitting condensation in an iron elbow. Fogel had become sensitive to his house, identifying with its creaks, its corners of decay, its irreversible expenditures of energy. He tried to study the section, the financial section. "THE DEFICIT PROBLEM—IS IT ALL IN OUR MINDS?" one headline read. Interest rates, restructuring, soft markets, debt, debt ...

He rested the paper on the floor beside his son's narrow bed and fell headlong asleep, while drizzle flecked the windowpanes and steam ticked in the radiators. He dreamed, in the deep colors of true weariness. Electricity wandered through his brain, activating now one set of memory cells and now another. A wash of buried emotion rounded these phantoms into light and shadow, and called up tears and outcries of indignation from Fogel's phantom self; he presided above the busy lit stage of his subconscious as prompter and playwright, audience and *deus ex machina* as well as hero. His parents hove into view—his father a coarse man, who worked with his hands, and his mother a virgin in her simplicity of mind, her narrow passion to defend as if sacred the little space her family had borrowed from the world. He hugged his pet teddy bear, Bruno. Bruno had a glass eye, on a long wire stem, like a toy flower. His parents were talking above him, urgently to each other, in a language he didn't know. In their vicinity, Fogel became heavy in every cell, so dense that he fell through into wakefulness, though the dream world tried to cling to his warm body, amid that unnatural ache of resurrection—the weight, the atrocious weight, of coming again to life!

His mouth felt parched, and a dribble from the downward corner of his lips had moistened the pillow. The air of the room was dusky. He did not at first know what room it was, of the many his long life had occupied. A fur of shadow had grown on every surface, even that of the sleek posters. The hour was indeterminate; yet Fogel knew at once that the day was still Easter.

How long had he slept, so solidly? Naps were not something he liked to do. Better to store up sleep, at his age, for the night. He listened for his wife's voice from their bedroom and heard nothing. He was frightened. He lay half curled up on the narrow bed like a fetus that has lost flexibility. A curve of terror chilled his abdomen, silvery and sore; had he been the phantom self of his dreams, he would have cried out aloud with the sensation. His eyes checked the items of the room—shiny posters, vacant fireplace, light plug, bookcase of abandoned schoolbooks, rack of obsolete cassettes, stolen NO PARKING sign, stuffed rabbit wearing a vest—one by one. Everything seemed still in place, yet something was immensely missing.

Guides to Reflection

1. How would you characterize what Easter has meant for Fogel?

2. Central to the story is Fogel's recall of a past affair, which ended at Eastertime decades before but has left him with a sense of sadness. How does this memory function in "Short Easter"?

3. Comment on the relevance of the following passage from Updike's memoir, *Self-Consciousness:* "During [my] adolescence, I reluctantly perceived of the Christian religion I had been born into that almost no one believed it, believed it really—not its ministers, nor its pillars like my father and his father before him. Though signs of belief (churches, public prayers, mottos on coins) existed everywhere, when you moved toward Christianity it disappeared, as fog solidly opaque in the distance thins to transparency when you walk into it."[1]

4. Updike says that when Fogel wakes from his nap, he finds himself caught in "the unnatural ache of resurrection" *(Reader, 19)*. Discuss what that "ache" might mean. Why is being born again to consciousness, so to speak, so "atrocious"?

5. Considering Fogel as a person in real distress—someone who has everything but senses that something is "immensely missing" *(Reader, 20)*—how as a Christian would you respond to him?

Notes

1. John Updike, *Self-Consciousness: Memoirs* (New York: Alfred A. Knopf, 1989), 230.

2

Anne Tyler

Readers of Anne Tyler's novels often comment on two distinctive aspects of her work: the frequency with which she creates unusual and sometimes zany characters, and the striking juxtaposition in her stories of tragedy and joy— of starkly sad things and quite funny things. The talkative dog trainer Muriel Pritchett in *The Accidental Tourist;* Morgan, a man of many hats, in *Morgan's Passing;* the fortune-teller Justine in *Searching for Caleb;* and the breathless Maggie Moran in *Breathing Lessons:* all mark their stories with their eccentricity, as do other memorable characters in each of Tyler's 13 novels. And yet, the hilarious moments these characters often engender—as when Edward the dog traps the dignified Charles Leary in the pantry despite Muriel's lessons or Maggie's many misadventures with cars—are set beside unhappy and even tragic moments—as when Jesse abandons Fiona and their baby in *Breathing Lessons* or when 10-year-old Ethan is shot dead by a robber in a fast food restaurant in *The Accidental Tourist.*

Asked about these distinctive features of her work, Tyler responded: "I write about those off-beat characters and that blend of laughter and tears because in my experience, that's what real life consists of."[1] Mixed through the complex, happy, and sad stories of "real life" that Tyler tells in her novels are her characters' struggles to make choices about their lives, to shape themselves, to construct workable if not always happy families, and to make sense of what happens to them.

In her 12th novel, *Saint Maybe* (1991), Tyler presents these themes in the life of the Bedloe family, who face a series of shocks: the sudden deaths of Danny, the elder son, and then of his wife, Lucy; the decision of the younger son, Ian, to adopt Lucy's children; and the "conversion" Ian experiences while listening to a storefront preacher—a dropout from an Episcopalian seminary who read the Bible and then left the seminary to found "The Church of the Second Chance" on a Baltimore street corner.

Before Danny's death, the Bedloes led a pleasant, quiet life on a short, quiet street. They were "Waverly Street's version of the ideal, apple-pie household: two amiable parents, three good-looking children, a dog, a cat, a scattering of goldfish."[2] The family's special quality was that they had a knack for easily overcoming the troubling things that happened to them; they absorbed, adapted, and went cheerfully on. Their short, one-block long street, "bracketed between a high stone cemetery wall at one end and the commercial clutter of Govans Road at the other"[3], surrounded them with kind, stable neighbors, unusual only in that one group was a continually changing set of foreigners—mostly Middle Easterners who were graduate students in engineering or medicine at Johns Hopkins University.

This steady world is shaken in a way the Bedloes cannot immediately absorb and overcome when Danny, slightly drunk, drives his car into the cemetery wall at the end of the street and kills himself. Some months later, his desperate widow takes an overdose of sleeping pills, leaving behind her three young children: seven-year-old Agatha, four-year-old Thomas, and the infant Daphne.

Ian, Danny's 18-year-old brother, is numb and guilt-ridden after these deaths. For Danny drove his car into the wall just after Ian blurted out his suspicions that Lucy, married to Danny less than a year, was unfaithful and—this suspicion seemingly incontrovertible—that Daphne was not Danny's child.

Burdened by his role in this series of tragedies, Ian leaves college, at first only temporarily to help his parents care for the orphaned children until their maternal relatives can be found. Walking the streets one evening, he passes "The Church of the Second Chance." He joins that evening's worship service, and then confesses his anguish to Reverend Emmett, who urges him to atone for what he has done. Ian decides to drop out of college and to join the church. Against his parents' wishes, he finds a job as a carpenter's apprentice and begins the task of rearing three children.

These initial events in *Saint Maybe* raise some deep and knotty questions that Tyler addresses in the rest of the novel. Particularly interesting is her treatment of Ian's religiosity. At first, it seems destined for an unsympathetic presentation. Ian joins what many people would consider an oddball group. The members of "The Church of the Second Chance" seem peculiar: calling each other "Sister" and "Brother"; doing good works together on Saturdays; avoiding alcohol, sugar, and caffeine; and worshiping frequently. Reverend Emmett seems presumptuous perhaps, telling Ian that he bears some responsibility to care for Lucy's children. Ian's religious commitment disturbs his parents and friends. How much, the readers wonder, does it disturb Anne Tyler? How much, in turn, will it disturb us?

In Tyler's earlier novels, religious characters appear occasionally. These characters, especially the clergy among them, often seem shallow, rigid, or unperceptive. The authors of two book-length studies of Tyler have termed her presentations of these clerics "humorous" and "satiric"[4] or even "scathing."[5] Tyler's portrayals of these fictional clerics, in addition to some critical public comments she has made about actual clerics, may lead readers to conclude that Tyler is unsympathetic to religion and religious people.[6] It is risky, though, to make very strong statements about Tyler's personal views on religious matters, or on many other topics. She grants few interviews, and then only through the mail. She refuses virtually all offers to make public appearances and so never faces the questioning those appearances often entail.[7]

The scarcity of her public comments makes a full understanding of her personal views on religion impossible. Tyler writes novels. Our interpretations of those novels, our responses to her characters and the ways she presents them, can be guides to our venturing hypotheses about her personal views. But these guides are all quite complex and ambiguous, and they leave considerable room for disagreement among readers. Readers may legitimately differ, for instance, on how sympathetic an author is to any particular character. And, even if they agree, a sympathetic portrayal of a cleric, for example, does not necessarily mean that the author is conventionally religious, nor does an unsympathetic portrayal necessarily suggest that she scorns religious people or their churches.

Whatever Tyler's personal views may now be, the shape of her own life must certainly have been influenced by her parents' strong religious convictions. Dedicated Quakers, Tyler's parents were active in Quaker communities in Minnesota and Illinois when Tyler was young. They joined utopian communities, first Coldbrook Farm in Pennsylvania and then, when she was seven years old, the Celo Community in North Carolina. A few years later, though, the family left Celo and settled in Raleigh where Tyler went to high school.[8]

The fervent religious convictions of Tyler's parents most likely marked Tyler's childhood in distinctive ways. Yet, her direct comments on her childhood and her religious perspectives are scarce. Tyler's silence turns us away from what she seems to find a potentially distracting curiosity about her life; it directs us toward her novels. In *Saint Maybe*, Tyler's most recent and her most extensive examination of religious themes, Ian's religiosity raises hard questions that sometimes cannot be answered; nonetheless, Tyler's portrayal of him and his religious conviction is full, rounded, and quite sympathetic.

Chapter 5 of *Saint Maybe*, entitled "People Who Don't Know the Answers," was published separately in *The New Yorker* shortly before the novel's publication in 1991. In this chapter, we see some of the consequences of Ian's religious commitment through the skeptical eyes of his father, Doug. Framing the chapter is the story of Doug's friendship with the foreigners who live across the street. At its center is the story of Doug's reluctant attendance, along with his wife, Bee, at a picnic sponsored by Ian's church. Both events tell of Doug's ventures into foreignness—the unpredictable, exotic, Middle Eastern world of his neighbors and the equally unpredictable and exotic world of his son's church. Both encounters prove good for Doug. The Middle Eastern graduate students distract and entertain him. They become his much-needed friends; they chat with him, consult him on their projects, and give him company. Being with the foreigners gives Doug glimpses of otherness and moments of familiar friendship that are intriguing, enlivening, and fun.

The church picnic brings Doug two important conversations: the first with the father of another young church member, and the second with Bee, his wife. The other church member's father is scornful of what he calls "The Church of the Second Rate," asking Doug: "Want to hear what I hate most about churches? They think they know the answers. I really hate that. It's the people who *don't* know the answers who are going to heaven, I tell you." To which the man's daughter replies: "But! ... The minute you say that, you see, you yourself become a person who knows the answers" *(Reader, 38)*. Neither the young woman's father nor Doug has anything to say in response. Riding in the car on the way home, Bee begins talking to Doug about Danny, their "golden boy," lamenting the downward slide of their lives since Danny's death: "We've had such extraordinary troubles," she said, "and somehow they've turned us ordinary" *(Reader, 41)*. Going to the church picnic brings Doug face to face with these two truths: the difficulty of knowing the answers and the ordinariness of suffering.

In the rest of the novel, Tyler explores the ramifications of these realities. She seems to be asking: What might happen to an ordinary man like Ian, who suffers and who doesn't know the answers, but who turns to God and, still not knowing all the answers, trusts his new convictions and lives his life accordingly?

Paula J. Carlson

Notes

1. Anne Tyler, interview quoted in *Understanding Anne Tyler* by Alice Hall Petry (Columbia: University of South Carolina Press, 1990), 6.

2. Anne Tyler, *Saint Maybe* (New York: Alfred A. Knopf, 1991), 4.

3. *Saint Maybe*, 3.

4. Elizabeth Evans, *Anne Tyler* (New York: Twayne Publishers, 1993), 79, 69.

5. *Understanding Anne Tyler*, 11.

6. *Anne Tyler*, x, and *Understanding Anne Tyler*, 11. In an interview Tyler said, "It's not that I have anything against ministers, but that I'm particularly concerned with how much right anyone has to change someone, and ministers are people who feel they have that right." Quoted in "An Interview with Anne Tyler" by Wendy Lamb, *Iowa Journal of Literary Studies* 3 (1981): 61.

7. *Understanding Anne Tyler*, 5.

8. *Anne Tyler*. Evans presents a short biography of Tyler on pages xiii-xv and 1-4.

People Who Don't Know the Answers

After Doug Bedloe retired, he had a little trouble thinking up things to do with himself. This took him by surprise, because he was accustomed to the schoolteacher's lengthy summer vacations and he'd never found it hard to fill them. But retirement, it seemed, was another matter. There wasn't any end to it. Also it was given more significance. Loaf around in summer, Bee would say he deserved his rest. Loaf in winter, she read it as pure laziness. "Don't you have someplace to go?" she asked him. "Lots of men join clubs or something. Couldn't you do Meals on Wheels? Volunteer at the hospital?"

Well, he tried. He approached a group at his church that worked with disadvantaged youths. Told them he had forty years' experience coaching baseball. They were delighted. First he was supposed to get some training, though—spend three Saturdays learning about the emotional ups and downs of adolescents. The second Saturday, it occurred to him he was tired of adolescents. He'd been dealing with their ups and downs for forty years now, and the fact was, they were shallow.

So then he enrolled in this night course in the modern short story (his daughter's idea). Figured *that* would not be shallow, and short stories were perfect since he never had been what you would call a speed reader. It turned out, though, he didn't have a knack for discussing things. You read a story; it's good or it's bad. What's to discuss? The other people in the class, they could ramble on forever. Halfway through the course, he just stopped attending.

He retreated to the basement, then. He built a toy chest for his youngest grandchild—a pretty decent effort, although Ian (Mr. Artsy-Craftsy) objected to particleboard. Also, carpentry didn't give him quite enough to think about. Left a kind of empty space in his mind that all sorts of bothersome notions could rush in and fill.

Once in a while something needed fixing; that was always welcome. Bee would bring him some household object and he would click his tongue happily and ask her, "What did you *do* to this?"

"I just broke it, Doug, all right?" she would say. "I deliberately went and broke it. I sat up late last night plotting how to break it."

And he would shake his head, feeling gratified and important.

Such occasions didn't arise every day, though, or even every week. Not nearly enough to keep him fully occupied.

It had been assumed all along that he would help out more with the grandkids, once he'd retired. Lord knows help was needed. Daphne was in first grade now but still a holy terror. Even the older two—ten and thirteen—took quite a lot of seeing to. And Bee's arthritis had all but crippled her and Ian was running himself ragged. They talked about getting a woman in a couple of days a week, but what with the cost of things ... well, money was a bit tight for that. So Doug tried to lend a hand, but he turned out to be kind of a dunderhead. For instance, he saw the kids had tracked mud across the kitchen floor and so he fetched the mop and bucket with the very best of intentions, but next thing he knew Bee was saying, "Doug, I swan, not to sweep first and swabbing all that dirty water around ..." and Ian said, "Here, Dad, I'll take over." Doug yielded the mop, feeling both miffed and relieved, and put on his jacket and whistled up the dog for a walk.

He and Beastie took long, long walks these days. Not long in distance but in time; Beastie was so old now she could barely creep. Probably she'd have preferred to stay home, but Doug would have felt foolish strolling the streets with no purpose. This gave him something to hang onto—her ancient, cracked leather leash, which sagged between them as she inched down the sidewalk. He could remember when she was a puppy and the leash grew taut as a clothesline every time a squirrel passed.

For no good reason, he pictured what it would look like if Bee were the one walking Beastie. The two of them hunched and arthritic, a matched set. It hurt to think of it. He had often seen such couples—aged widows and their decrepit pets. If he died, Bee would *have* to walk Beastie, at least in the daytime when the kids weren't home. But of course, he was not about to die. He had always kept in shape. His hair might be gray now but it was still there, and he could fit into trousers he'd bought thirty years ago.

A while back, though, their family doctor had told him something unsettling. He'd said, "Know what I hate? When a patient comes in and says, 'Doc, I'm here for a checkup. Next month I hit retirement age and I've planned all these great adventures.' Then sure as shooting, I'll find he's got something terminal. It never fails."

Well, Doug had avoided *that* eventuality. He just hadn't gone for a checkup.

And anyhow, planned no great adventures.

The trouble was, he was short on friends. Why had he never noticed before? It seemed he'd had so many back in high school and college.

If Danny had lived, maybe he would have been a friend.

Although Ian was nice company too, of course.

It was just that Ian seemed less ... oh, less related to him, somehow. Maybe on account of that born-again business. He was so serious and he never just goofed off the way Danny used to do or sat around shooting the breeze with his dad. Didn't even have a girlfriend anymore; that pretty little Cicely had faded clear out of the picture. She had found someone else, Doug supposed. Not that Ian had ever said so. That was the thing: they didn't talk.

Danny used to talk.

Walking Beastie past the foreigners' house one unseasonably mild day in February, Doug noticed someone lying face down on the roof. Good Lord, what now? They lived the strangest lives over there. This fellow was sprawled parallel to the eaves, poking some wire or electrical cord through an upstairs window. Doug paused to watch. Beastie groaned and thudded to the ground. "Need help?" Doug called.

The foreigner raised his head. In that peremptory way that foreigners sometimes have, he said, "Yes, please to enter the house and accept this wire."

"Oh. Okay," Doug said.

He let Beastie's leash drop. She wasn't going anywhere.

He had been in the foreigners' house several times, because they gave a neighborhood party every Fourth of July. ("Happy your Independence Day," one of them had once said. "Happy *yours*," he'd answered before he thought.) He knew that the window in question belonged to the second-floor bathroom, and so he crossed the hall, which was totally bare of furniture, and climbed the stairs and entered the bathroom. The foreigner's face hung upside down outside the window, his thick black hair standing straight off his head so that he looked astonished. "Here!" he called.

Darned if he hadn't broken a corner out of a pane. Not a neatly drilled hole in the wood but a jagged triangle in the glass itself. A wire poked through—antenna wire, it looked like. Doug pulled on it carefully so as not to abrade it. He reeled it in foot by foot. "Okay," the foreigner said, and his face disappeared.

Doug hadn't thought to wonder how the man had got up on the roof in the first place. All at once he was down again, brushing off his clothes in the bathroom doorway—a good-looking, stocky young fellow in a white shirt and blue jeans. You could always tell foreigners by the way they wore their jeans, so neat and proper with the waist at the actual waistline, and in this man's case even a crease ironed in. Jim, was that his name? No, Jim was from an earlier batch. (The foreigners came and went in rotation, with their M.D.'s or their Ph.D.'s or their engineering degrees.) "Frank?" Doug tried.

"Fred."

They were always so considerate about dropping whatever unpronounceable names they'd been christened with. Or not christened, maybe, but—

"Please to tie the wire about the radiator's paw," Fred told him.

"What is it, anyhow?"

"It is aerial for mv shortwave radio."

"Ah."

"I attached it to TV antenna on chimney.

"Is that safe?" Doug asked him.

"Maybe; maybe not," Fred said cheerfully.

Doug wouldn't have worried, except these people seemed prone to disasters. Last summer, while hooking up an intercom, they had set their attic on fire. Doug wasn't sure how an intercom could start a fire exactly. All he knew was, smoke had begun billowing from the little eyebrow window on the roof and then six or seven foreigners had sauntered out of the house and stood in the yard gazing upward, looking interested. Finally Mrs. Jordan had called the fire department. What on earth use would they have for an intercom anyway? she had asked Bee later. But that was how they were, the foreigners: they just loved gadgets.

Fred was walking backwards now, playing out the wire as he headed across the hall. From the looks of things, he planned to let it lie in the middle of the floor where it would ambush every passerby. "You got any staples?" Doug asked, following.

"Excuse me?"

"Staples? U-shaped nails? Electrical staples, insulated," Doug went on, without a hope in this world. "You tack the wire to the baseboard so it doesn't trip folks up."

"Maybe later," Fred said vaguely.

Meanwhile leading the wire directly across the hall and allowing not one inch of slack.

In Fred's bedroom, gold brocade draped an army cot. A bookcase displayed folded T-shirts, boxer shorts, and rolled socks stacked in a pyramid like cannonballs. Doug managed to take all this in because there was nothing else to look at—not a desk or chair or bureau, not a mirror or family photo. A brown plastic radio sat on the windowsill, and Fred inserted the wire into a hole in its side.

"Looks to me like you might've brought the wire in *this* window," Doug told him.

But Fred shrugged and said, "More far to fall."

"Oh," Doug said.

Presumably, Fred was not one of the engineering students.

Fred turned on the radio and music started playing, some Middle Eastern tune without an end or a beginning. He half closed his eyes and nodded his head to the beat.

"Well, I'd better be going," Doug said.

"You know what means these words?" Fred asked. "A young man is telling farewell to his sweetheart, he is saying to her now—"

"Gosh, Beastie must be wondering where I've got to," Doug said. "I'll just see myself out, never mind."

He had thought it would be a relief to escape the music, but after he left—after he returned home, even, and unsnapped Beastie's leash—the tune continued to wind through his head, blurred and wandery and mysteriously exciting.

A couple of days later, the foreigners tried wiring the radio to speakers set strategically around the house. The reason Doug found out about it was, Fred came over to ask what those U-shaped nails were called again. "Staples," Doug told him, standing at the door in his slippers.

"No, no. Staples are for paper," Fred said firmly.

"But the nails are called staples too. See, what you want is ..." Doug said, and then he said, "Wait here. I think I may have some down in the basement."

So one thing led to another. He found the staples, he went over to help, he stayed for a beer afterward, and before long he was more or less hanging out there. They always had some harebrained project going, something he could assist with or (more often) advise them not to attempt; and because they were students, keeping students' irregular hours, he could generally count on finding at least a couple of them at home. Five were currently living there: Fred, Ray, John, John Two, and Ollie. On weekends more arrived—fellow countrymen studying elsewhere—and some of the original five disappeared. Doug left them alone on weekends. He preferred late weekday afternoons, when the smells of spice and burnt onions had already started rising from Ollie's blackened saucepans in the kitchen and the others lolled in the living room with their beers. The living room was furnished with two webbed aluminum beach lounges, a wrought-iron lawn chair, and a box spring propped on four stacks of faded textbooks. Over the fireplace hung a wrinkled paper poster of a belly dancer drinking a Pepsi. A collapsible metal TV tray held the telephone, and the wall above it was scribbled all over with names and numbers and Middle Eastern curlicues. Doug liked that idea—that a wall could serve as a phone directory. It struck him as very practical. He would squint at the writing until it turned lacy and decorative, and then he'd take another sip of beer.

These people weren't much in the way of drinkers. They appeared to view alcohol as yet another inscrutable American convention, and they would dangle their own beers politely, forgetting them for long minutes; so Doug never had more than one. Then he'd say, "Well, back to the fray," and they would rise to see him off, thanking him once again for whatever he'd done.

At home, by comparison, everything seemed so permanent—the rooms layered over with rugs and upholstered furniture and framed pictures. The grandchildren added layers of their own; the hall was awash in cast-off jackets and schoolbooks. Bee would be in the kitchen starting supper. (How unadorned the Bedloes' suppers smelled! Plain meat, boiled vegetables, baked potatoes.) And if Ian was back from work he'd be occupied with the kids—sorting out whose night it was to set the table, arbitrating their disputes or even taking part in them as if he were a kid himself. Listen to him with Daphne, for instance. She was nagging him to find her green sweater; tomorrow was St. Patrick's Day. "Your green sweater's in the wash," he said, and that should have been the end of it—would have been, if Bee had been in charge. But Daphne pressed on, wheedling. "Please? Please, Ian? They'll make fun of me if I don't wear something green."

"Tell them your eyes are the something green."

"My what? My eyes? But they're blue."

"Well, if anybody points that out, put on this injured look and say, 'Oh. I've always liked to *think* of them as green.'"

"Oh, Ian," Daphne said. "You're such a silly."

He was, Doug reflected. And a sucker besides. For sure enough, later that night he heard the washing machine start churning.

Most days Ian took the car, but Tuesdays he caught the bus to work so Doug could drive Bee to the doctor. She had to go every single week. Doug knew that doctor's waiting room so well by now that he could see it in his dreams. A leggy, wan philodendron plant hung over the vinyl couch. A table was piled with magazines you would have to be desperate to read—densely printed journals devoted to infinitesimal research findings.

Two other doctors shared the office: a dermatologist and an ophthalmologist. One morning Doug saw the ophthalmologist talking with a very attractive young woman at the receptionist's desk. The receptionist must have proposed some time or date, because the young woman shook her head and said, "I'm sorry, I can't make it then."

"Can't make it?" the doctor asked. "This is surgery, not a hair appointment. We're talking about your eyesight!"

"I'm busy that day," the young woman said.

"Miss Wilson, maybe you don't understand. This is the kind of problem you take care of *now*, you take care of *yesterday*. Not next week or next month. I can't state that too strongly."

"Yes, but I happen to be occupied that day," the young woman said.

Then Bee came out of Dr. Plumm's office, and Doug didn't get to hear the end of the conversation. He kept thinking about it, though. What could make a person defer such crucial surgery? She was meeting a lover? But she could always meet him another day. She'd be fired from her job? But no employer was *that* hard-hearted. Nothing Doug came up with was sufficient explanation.

Imagine being so offhand about your eyesight. About your life, was what it amounted to. As if you wouldn't have to endure the consequences forever and ever after.

Wednesday their daughter dropped by to help with the heavier cleaning. She breezed in around lunchtime with a casserole for supper and a pair of stretchy gloves she'd heard would magically ease arthritic fingers. "Ordinary department-store gloves, I saw this last night on the evening news," she told Bee. "You're lucky I got them when I did; I went to Hochschild's. Don't you know there'll be a big rush for them."

"Yes, dear, that was very nice of you," Bee said dutifully. She already owned gloves, medically prescribed, much more official than these were. Still, she put these on and spread her hands out as flat as possible, testing. She was wearing one of Ian's sweatshirts and baggy slacks and slipper-socks. In the gloves, which were the dainty, white, lady's-tea kind, she looked a little bit crazy.

Claudia filled a bucket in the kitchen sink and added a shot of ammonia. "Going to tackle that chandelier," she told them. "I noticed it last week. A *disgrace!*"

Probably it was Ian's housekeeping she was so indignant with—or just time itself, time that had coated each prism with dust. She wasn't thinking how it sounded to waltz into a person's home and announce that it was filthy. Doug cast a sideways glance at Bee to see how she was taking it. Her eyes were teary, but that could have been the ammonia. He waited till Claudia had left the kitchen, sloshing her bucket into the dining room, and then he laid a hand on top of Bee's. "Peculiar, isn't it?" he said. "First you're scolding your children and then all at once they're so smart they're scolding *you.*"

Bee smiled, and he saw that they weren't real tears after all. "I suppose," he went on more lightly, "there was some stage when we were equals. I mean while she was on the rise and we were on the downslide. A stage when we were level with each other.

"Well, I must have been on the phone at the time," Bee said, and then she laughed.

Her hand in the glove felt dead to him, like his own hand after he'd slept on it wrong and cut off the circulation.

The foreigners set their car on fire, trying to install a radio. "I didn't know radios were flammable," Mrs. Jordan said, watching from the Bedloes' front porch. Doug was a bit surprised himself, but then electronics had never been his strong point. He went over to see if he could help. The car was a Dodge from the late fifties or maybe early sixties, whenever it was that giant fins were all the rage. Once the body had been powder blue but now it was mostly a deep, matte red from rust, and one door was white and one fender turquoise. Whom it belonged to was unclear, since the foreigner who had bought it, second- or third-hand, had long since gone back to his homeland.

John Two and Fred and Ollie were standing around the car in graceful poses, languidly fanning their faces. The smoke appeared to be coming from the dashboard. Doug said, "Fellows? Think we should call the fire department?" but Fred said, "Oh, we dislike to keep disturbing them."

Hoping nothing would explode, Doug reached through the open window on the driver's side and pulled the first wire his fingers touched. Almost immediately the smoke thinned. There was a strong smell of burning rubber, but no real damage—at least none that he could see. It was hard to tell; the front seat was worn to bare springs and the backseat had been removed altogether.

"Maybe we just won't have radio," John Two told Ollie.

"We never had radio before," Fred said.

"We were very contented," John Two said, "and while we traveled we could hear the birds sing."

Doug pictured them traveling through a flat green countryside like the landscape in a child's primer. They would be the kind who set off without filling the gas tank first or checking the tire pressure, he was certain. Chances were they wouldn't even have a road map.

One morning when he came downstairs he found Beastie dead on the kitchen floor, her body not yet stiff. It was a shock, although he should have been prepared for it. She was sixteen years old. He could still remember what she'd looked like when they brought her home—small enough to fit in her own feed dish. That first winter it had snowed and snowed, and she had humped her fat little body ecstatically through the drifts like a Slinky toy, with a dollop of snow icing her nose and snowflakes on her lashes.

He went upstairs to wake Ian. He wanted to get her buried before the children saw her. "Ian," he said. "Son."

Ian's room still looked so boyish. Model airplanes sat on the shelves among autographed baseballs and high-school yearbooks. The bedspread was printed with antique cars. It could have been one of those rooms that's maintained as a shrine after a young person dies.

Danny's room, on the other hand, had been redecorated for Thomas. Not a trace of Danny remained.

"Son?"

"Hmm."

"I need you to help me bury Beastie."

Ian opened his eyes. "Beastie?"

"I found her this morning in the kitchen."

Ian considered a moment and then sat up. When Doug was sure he was awake, he left the room and went downstairs for his jacket.

Beastie had not been a large dog, but she weighed a lot. Doug heaved her onto the doormat and then dragged the mat outside and down the back steps. Thump, thump, thump—it made him wince. The mat left a trail in the sparkling grass. He backed up to the azalea and dropped the corners of the mat and straightened. It was six thirty or so—too early for the neighbors to be about yet. The light was nearly colorless, the traffic noises sparse and distant.

Ian came out with his windbreaker collar turned up. He had both shovels with him. "Good thing the ground's not frozen," Doug told him.

"Right."

"This is probably not even legal, anyhow."

They chipped beneath the sod, trying as best they could not to break it apart, and laid it to one side. A breeze was ruffling Beastie's fur and Doug kept imagining that she could feel it, that she was aware of what they were doing. He made his mind a blank. He set up an alternating rhythm with Ian, hacking through the reddish earth and occasionally ringing against a pebble or a root. In spite of the breeze he started sweating and he stopped to take off his jacket, but Ian kept his on. Ian didn't look hot at all; he looked chilly and pale, with that fine white line around his lips that meant he had his jaw set. For the first time, Doug thought to wonder how this was hitting him. "Guess you'll miss her," he said.

"Yes," Ian said, still digging.

"Beastie's been around since you were ... what? Eight or so, or not even that.

Ian nodded and bent to toss a rock out of the way.

"We'll let the kids set some kind of marker up," Doug told him. "Plant bulbs or something. Make it pretty."

It was all he could think of to offer.

They ended up cheating a bit on the grave—dug more of an oval than a rectangle, so they had to maneuver to get her into it. She fit best on her side, slightly curled. When Doug saw her velvety snout against the clay, tears came to his eyes. She had always been such an undemanding dog, so accommodating, so adaptable. "Ah, God," he said, and then he looked up and realized Ian was praying. His head was bowed and his lips were moving. Doug hastily bowed his own head. He felt as if Ian were the grownup and he the child. It had been years, maybe all the years of his adulthood, since he had relied so thankfully on someone else's knowledge of what to do.

The two younger children came down with chicken pox—first Daphne and then Thomas. Everybody waited for Agatha to get it too but she must have had it earlier, before they knew her. Daphne was hardly sick at all, but Thomas had a much worse case and one night he woke up delirious. Doug heard his hoarse, startled voice, oddly bright in the darkness—"Don't let them come! Don't let their sharp hooves!"—and then Ian's steady "Thomas, old man. Thomas. Tom-Tom."

In that short-story course, Doug had read a story about an experiment conducted by creatures from outer space. What the creatures wanted to know was, could earthlings form emotional attachments? Or were they merely at the mercy of biology? So they cut a house in half in the middle of the night, and they switched it with another half house in some totally different location. Tossed the two households together like so many game pieces. This woman woke up with a man and some children she'd never laid eyes on before. Naturally she was terribly puzzled and upset, and the others were too, but as it happened the children had some kind of illness, measles or something (maybe even chicken pox, come to think of it), and so of course she did everything she could to make them comfortable. The creatures' conclusion, therefore, was that earthlings didn't discriminate. Their family feelings, so called, were a matter of blind circumstance.

Doug couldn't remember now how the story had ended. Maybe that *was* the end. He couldn't quite recollect.

In the dark, Bee's special white arthritis gloves glowed eerily. She lay on her side, facing him, with the gloves curled beneath her chin. The slightest sound used to wake her when their own three children were little—a cough or even a whimper. Now she slept through everything, and Doug was glad. It was a pity so much rested on Ian, but Ian was young. He had the energy.

He hadn't reached the point yet where it just plain didn't seem worth the effort.

Ian invited his parents to a Christian Fellowship Picnic. "To a what?" Doug asked, stalling for time. (Who cared what it was called? It was bound to be something embarrassing.)

"Each of us invites people we'd like to join in fellowship with," Ian said in that deadly earnest way he had. "People who aren't members of our congregation."

"I thought that church of yours didn't believe in twisting folkses' arms."

"It doesn't. We don't. This is only for fellowship."

They were watching the evening news—Doug, Bee, and Ian. Now Bee looked away from a skyful of bomber airplanes to say, "I've never understood what people mean by 'fellowship.'"

"Just getting together, Mom. Nothing very mysterious."

"Then why even say it? Why not say 'getting together'?"

Ian didn't take offense. He said, "Reverend Emmett wants us to ask, oh, people we care about and people who wonder what we believe and people who might feel hostile to us."

"We're not hostile!"

"Then maybe you would qualify for one of the other groups," Ian said mildly.

Bee looked at Doug. Doug pulled himself together (he had a sense of struggling toward the surface) and said, "Isn't it sort of early for a picnic? We're still getting frost at night!"

"This is an indoor picnic," Ian told him.

"Then what's the point?"

"Reverend Emmett's mother, Sister Priscilla, has relatives out in the valley who own a horse farm. They're in Jamaica for two weeks and they told her she could stay in the house."

"Did they say she could throw a church picnic in the house?"

"We won't do any harm."

Bee was still looking at Doug. (She wanted him to say no, of course.) The bombers had given way to a moisturizer commercial.

"Well, it's nice of you to think of us, son," Doug said, "but—"

"I've invited Mrs. Jordan, too."

"Mrs. Jordan?"

"Right."

"*Jessie* Jordan?"

"She's always wanting to know what Second Chance is all about."

This put a whole different light on things. How could they refuse when a mere neighbor had accepted? Drat Jessie Jordan, with her lone-woman eagerness to go anywhere she was asked!

And then she had the nerve to make out she was being so daring, so rakish. On the way to Greenspring Valley (for they did end up attending, taking their own car which was easier on Bee's hips than the bus), Mrs. Jordan bounced and burbled like a six-year-old. "Isn't this exciting?" she said. She was dressed as if headed for a Buckingham Palace garden party—cartwheel hat ringed with flowers, swishy silk dress beneath her drab winter coat. "You know, there are so many alternative religions springing up these days," she said. "I worry I'll fall hopelessly behind."

"And wouldn't *that* be a shame," Bee said sourly. She wore an ordinary gray sweat suit, not her snazzy warm-up suit with the complicated zippers; so her hands must be giving her trouble today. Doug himself was dressed as if for golfing, carefully color-coordinated to compensate for what might be misread as sloppiness on Bee's part. He kept the car close behind Second Chance's rented bus. Sometimes Daphne's little thumbtack of a face bobbed up in the bus's rear window, smiling hugely and mouthing elaborate messages no one could catch. "*What* did she say? What?" Bee asked irritably.

"Can't quite make it out, hon."

They traveled deeper and deeper into country that would be luxurious in the summer but was now a vast network of bare branches lightly tinged with green. Pasturelands extended for miles. The driveway they finally turned into was too long to see to the end, and the white stone house was larger than some hotels. "Oh! Would you look!" Mrs. Jordan cried, clapping her hands.

Doug didn't like to admit it, but he felt easier about Second Chance now that he saw such a substantial piece of property connected to it. He wondered if the relatives were members themselves. Probably not, though.

They parked on the paved circle in front. Passengers poured from the bus—first the children, then the grownups. Doug fancied he could tell the members from the visitors. The members had a dowdy, worn, slumping look; the visitors were dressier and full of determined gaiety.

It occurred to him that Bee could be mistaken for a member.

Carrying baskets, coolers, and Thermos jugs, everyone followed Reverend Emmett's mother up the flagstone walk. They entered the front hall with its slate floor and center staircase, and several people said, "Ooh!"

"Quite a joint," Doug murmured to Bee.

Bee hushed him with a look.

They crossed velvety rugs and gleaming parquet and finally arrived in an enormous sun porch with a long table at its center and modern, high-gloss chairs and lounges set all about. "The conservatory," Reverend Emmett's mother said grandly. She was a small, finicky woman in a matched sweater set and a string of pearls and a pair of chunky jeans that seemed incongruous, downright wrong, as if she'd forgotten to change into the bottom half of her outfit. "Let's spread our picnic," she said. "Emmett, did you bring the tablecloth?"

"I thought you were bringing that."

"Well, never mind. Just put my potato salad here at this end.

Reverend Emmett wore a sporty polo shirt, a tan windbreaker, and black dress trousers. (He and his mother belonged in Daphne's block set, the one where you mismatch heads and legs and torsos.) He put a covered bowl where she directed, and then the others laid out platters of fried chicken, tubs of coleslaw, and loaves of home-baked bread. The table—varnished so heavily that it seemed wet—gradually disappeared. Streaky squares of sunlight from at least a dozen windows warmed the room, and people started shedding their coats and jackets. "Dear Lord in heaven," Reverend Emmett said (catching Doug with one arm half out of a sleeve), "the meal is a bountiful gift from Your hands and the company is more so. We thank You for this joyous celebration. Amen."

It was true there was something joyous in the atmosphere. Everyone converged upon the food, clucking and exclaiming. The children turned wild. Even Agatha, ponderously casual in a ski sweater and stirrup pants, pushed a boy back with shy enthusiasm when he gave her a playful nudge at the punch bowl. The members steered the guests magnanimously toward the choice dishes; they took on a proprietary air as they pointed out particular features of the house. "Notice the leaded panes," they said, as if they themselves were intimately familiar with them. The guests (most as suspicious as Doug and Bee, no doubt) showed signs of thawing. "Why, this is not bad," one silver-haired man said—the father, Doug guessed, of the hippie-type girl at his elbow. Doug had hold of too much dinner now to shake hands, but he nodded at the man and said, "How do. Doug Bedloe."

"Mac McClintock," the man said. "You just visiting?"

"Right."

"His son is Brother Ian," the hippie told her father. "I just think Brother Ian is so faithful," she said to Doug.

"Well ... thanks."

"My daughter Gracie," Mac said. "Have you met?"

"No, I don't believe we have."

"We've met!" Gracie said. "I'm the one who fetched your grandchildren from school every day when your wife was in the hospital."

"Oh, yes," Doug said. He didn't have the faintest memory of it.

"I fetched the children for Brother Ian and then Brother Ian closed up the rat holes in my apartment."

"Really," Doug said.

"My daughter lives in a slum," Mac told him.

"Now, Daddy."

"She makes less money than I made during the Depression and then she gives it all to this Church of the Second Rate."

"Second Chance! And I do not; I tithe. I don't have to do even that, if I don't want to. It's all in secret; we don't believe in public collection. You act like they're defrauding me or something."

"They're a church, aren't they? A church'll take its people for whatever it can get," Mac said. He glanced at Doug. "Hope that doesn't offend you."

"Me? No, no."

"Want to hear what I hate most about churches? They think they know the answers. I really hate that. It's the people who *don't* know the answers who are going to heaven, I tell you."

"But!" his daughter said. "The minute you say that, you see, you yourself become a person who knows the answers."

Mac gave Doug an exasperated look and chomped into a drumstick.

Bee was sitting on a chaise lounge with her legs stretched out, sharing a plate with Daphne. She was the only guest who seemed to have remained outside the gathering. Everyone else was laughing, growing looser, circulating from group to group in a giddy, almost tipsy way. (Although of course there wasn't a bit of alcohol; just that insipid fruit punch.) Reverend Emmett was holding forth on his inspiration for this picnic. "I felt led," he told a circle of women. He had the breathless look of an athlete being interviewed after a triumph. "I was listening to one of our brothers a couple of weeks ago; he said he wished he could share his salvation with his parents except they never would agree to come to services. And all at once I felt led to say, 'Why should it be services? Why not a picnic?'"

The women smiled and nodded and their glasses flashed. (One of them was Jessie Jordan, looking thrilled.) An extremely fat young woman threaded her way through the crowd with a plastic garbage bag, saying, "Plates? Cups? Keep your forks, though. Dessert is on its way."

What could they serve for dessert if they didn't believe in sugar? Fruit salad, it turned out, in little foil dishes. Thomas carried one of the trays around. When he came to Doug he said, "Grandpa? Are you having a good time?"

"Oh, yes."

"Are you making any friends?"

"Certainly," Doug said, and he felt a sudden wrench for the boy's thin, anxious face with its dots of old chicken-pox scars. He took a step closer to Mac McClintock, although they'd run out of small talk some minutes ago.

The women were clearing the table now, debating leftovers.

"It seems a shame to throw all this out."

"Won't you take it home?"

"No, you."

"Law, I couldn't eat it in a month of Sundays."

"We wouldn't want to waste it, though."

Reverend Emmett's mother said, "Mr. Bedloe, we all think so highly of Brother Ian."

"Thank you," Doug said. This was starting to remind him of Parents' Night at elementary school. He swallowed a chunk of canned pineapple, which surely contained sugar, didn't it? "And you must be very proud of *your* son," he added.

"Yes, I am," she said. "I look around me and I see so many people, so many redeemed people, and I think, 'If not for Emmett, what would they be doing?'"

What *would* they be doing? Most would be fine, Doug supposed—his own son among them. Lord, yes. But in all fairness, he supposed this church met a real need for some others. And so he looked around too, following Sister What's-Her-Name's eyes. What he saw, though, was not what he had expected. Instead of the festive throng he had been watching a few minutes ago, he saw a spreading circle of stillness that radiated from the table and extended now even to the children, so that a cluster of little girls in one corner allowed their jack ball to die and the boys gave up their violent ride in the glider. Even Bee seemed galvanized, an orange section poised halfway to her parted lips.

"It's the table," a woman told Reverend Emmett's mother.

"The—?"

"Something's damaged the surface."

Reverend Emmett's mother thrust her way through the circle of women, actually shoving one aside. Doug craned to see what they were talking about. The table was bare now and even shinier than before; someone had wiped it with a damp cloth. It looked perfect, at first glance, but then when he tilted his head to let the light slant differently he saw that the shine was marred at one end by several distinct, unshiny rings.

"Oh, no," Reverend Emmett's mother breathed.

Everyone started speaking at once: "Try mayonnaise."

"Try toothpaste."

"Rub it down with butter."

"Quiet! Please!" Reverend Emmett's mother said. She closed her eyes and pressed both hands to her temples.

Reverend Emmett stood near Doug, peering over the others' heads.

(Above the collar of his jaunty polo shirt, his neck looked scrawny and pathetic.) "Perhaps," he said, "if we attempted to—"

"Shut up and let me *think*, Emmett!"

Silence.

"Maybe if I came back tomorrow," she said finally, "with that cunning little man from Marx Antiques, the one who restores old ... he could strip it and refinish it. Don't you suppose? But the owners are due home Tuesday, and if he has to strip the whole ... but never mind! I'll tell him to work round the clock! Or I'll ask if ..."

More silence.

Ian said, "Was it soaped?"

Everyone turned and looked for him. It took a minute to find him; he was standing at the far end of the room.

"Seems to me the finish is some kind of polyurethane," he said, "and if those rings are grease, well, a little soap wouldn't do any harm and it might even—"

"Soap! Yes!" Reverend Emmett's mother said.

She went herself to the kitchen. While she was gone, the fat young woman told Doug, "Brother Ian works with wood every day, you know."

"Yes, I'm his father," Doug said.

She said, "Are you really!"

Reverend Emmett's mother came back. She held a sponge and a bottle of liquid detergent. They parted to let her through and she approached the table and bent over it. Doug was too far away to see what she did next, but he heard the sighs of relief. "Now dry it off," someone suggested.

A woman whipped a paisley scarf from her neck and offered that, and it was accepted.

"Perfect," someone said.

This time when he craned, Doug saw that the rings had vanished.

Right away the congregation started packing, collecting coats and baskets. Maybe they would have anyhow, but Doug thought he detected a sort of letdown in the general mood. People filed out meekly, not glancing back at the house as they left it. (Doug imagined the house thinking, *Goodness, what was all THAT about?*) They crossed the columned front porch with their heads lowered. Doug helped Bee into the car. "Coming?" he asked Mrs. Jordan.

"Oh, I'm going to ride in the bus," she said. She alone seemed undampened. "Wasn't Ian the hero, though!"

"Sure thing," Doug said.

He watched her set off toward the bus with one hand clamping down her cartwheel hat.

Driving home, he made no attempt to stay with the others. He left the bus behind on the Beltway and breezed eastward at a speed well above the legal limit. "So now we've been to a Christian Fellowship Picnic," he told Bee.

"Yes," she said.

"I wonder if it'll become a yearly event."

"Probably," she said.

Then she started talking about Danny. How did she get from the picnic to Danny? No telling. She started kneading the knuckles of her right hand, the hand that looked more swollen, and she said, "Sometimes I have the strangest feeling. I give this start and I think, 'Why!' I think, 'Why, here we are! Just going about our business the same as usual!' And yet so much has changed. Danny is gone, our golden boy, our first baby boy that we were so proud of, and our house is stuffed with someone else's children. You know they *all* are someone else's. You know that! And Ian is a whole different person and Claudia's so bustling now and our lives have turned so makeshift and second-class, so second-string, so second-fiddle, and everything's been lost. Isn't it amazing that we keep on going? That we keep on shopping for clothes and getting hungry and laughing at jokes on TV? When our oldest son is dead and gone and we'll never see him again and our life's in ruins!"

"Now, sweetie," he said.

"We've had such extraordinary troubles," she said, "and somehow they've turned us ordinary. That's what's so hard to figure. We're not a special family anymore."

"Why, sweetie, of course we're special," he said.

"We've turned uncertain. We've turned into worriers."

"Bee, sweetie."

"Isn't it amazing?"

It was astounding, if he thought about it. But he was careful not to.

The weather began to grow warmer, and Doug raised all the windows and lugged the summer clothing down from the attic for Bee. Across the street, the foreigners came out in their shirtsleeves to install an electric garage-door opener they'd ordered from a catalog. Doug found this amusing. A door that opened on its own, for a car that could barely *move* on its own! Of course he kept them company while they worked, but the door in question was solid wood and very heavy, potentially lethal, and he'd just as soon not be standing under it when calamity struck. He stayed several feet away, watching Ollie teeter on a kitchen chair as he screwed something to a rafter overhead. Then when Doug got bored he ambled inside with the two who were less mechanically inclined, leaving Ollie and Fred and John Two to carry on. He refused a beer (it was ten in the morning) but accepted a seat by the window, where a light breeze stirred the tattered paper shade.

From here the garage was invisible, since it lay even with the front of the house, but he could see Fred standing in the drive with the pushbutton control in both hands, pressing hard and then harder. Doug grinned. Fred leaned forward, his face a mask of straining muscle, and he bore down on the button with all his might. You didn't have to set eyes on the door to know it wasn't reacting. Meanwhile Ollie walked out to the street and climbed into the car and started the engine, and John Two removed a brick from under the left rear wheel. Optimistic of them; Doug foresaw a good deal more work before the garage would be ready for an occupant. Through the open window he heard the croupy putt-putt as the car turned in and rolled up the drive and sat idling. "In another catalog," John One was saying, "we have seen remarkable invention: automatic yard lights! That illuminate when dark falls! We plan to send away for them immediately."

"I can hardly wait," Doug said, and then he twisted in his chair because he thought he noticed someone emerging from his own house, but it was only shrubbery stirring in the breeze.

He was a touch nearsighted, and the mesh of the window screen seemed more distinct to him than what lay beyond it. What lay beyond it—home— had the blocky, blurred appearance of something worked in needlepoint, each tiny square in the screen filled with a square of color. Not only was there a needlepoint house but also a needlepoint car out front, a needlepoint swing on the porch, a needlepoint bicycle in the yard. His entire little world: a cozy, old-fashioned sampler stitched in place forever.

The best thing about the foreigners, he decided, was how they thought living in America was a story they were reading, or a movie they were watching. It was happening to someone else; it wasn't theirs. Good Lord, not even their names were theirs. Here they spoke lines invented by other people, not genuine language—not the language that simply *is,* with no need for translation. Here they wore blue denim costumes and inhabited a Hollywood set complete with make-believe furniture. But when they went back home, there they'd behave as seriously as anyone. They would fall in love and marry and have children and they'd agonize over their children's problems, and struggle to get ahead, and practice their professions soberly and efficiently. What Doug was witnessing was only a brief holiday from their real lives.

He was pleased by this notion. He thought he'd examine it further later on—consider, say, what happened to those foreigners who ended up *not* going home. The holiday couldn't last forever, could it? Was there a certain moment when the movie set turned solid? But for now, he didn't bother himself with all that. He was happy just to sit here, letting some of their Time Out rub off on him.

Then Ollie turned toward the house and called, "Come see!" and for courtesy's sake, Doug rose and followed Ray and John One to the yard. Other neighbors were here too, he realized. It looked like a party. He joined them and stood squinting in the sunshine, smiling at the foreigners' car which sat half inside the garage and half out like a crumpled beer can, with the door bisecting it neatly across the middle.

Guides to Reflection

1. The Bedloes's dog, Beastie, dies in the course of this chapter of *Saint Maybe*. Ian prays at the grave he and Doug dig for her in the backyard. Despite his antipathy to Ian's church, Doug is quite relieved when Ian prays. Why do you think Doug reacts this way to Ian's silent prayer?

2. Doug is shocked when he overhears a conversation in the waiting room at a doctor's office. An ophthalmologist is energetically trying to persuade a patient not to delay treatment, but the patient brushes the doctor off. Doug thinks: "Imagine being so offhand about your eyesight. About your life, was what it amounted to. As if you wouldn't have to endure the consequences forever and ever after" *(Reader, 31)*. How do the Bedloes seem to be enduring the consequences of the choices they have made?

3. In the short fiction course he takes, Doug reads a science fiction story about aliens who study human emotions by bisecting two houses and switching halves of families. The strangers quickly form new familial groups. The Bedloe family is just such an odd mix. What can you conclude about their "family feelings" *(Reader, 34)* in "People Who Don't Know the Answers"?

4. The visitors at the church picnic have varying reactions to the Church of the Second Chance. The reactions range from Mrs. Jordan's curiosity to Doug's embarrassment to Mac's hostility. What does Tyler's view of these various responses seem to be? What is yours?

5. At the picnic, Doug surmises that everyone who belongs to the Church of the Second Chance would be doing just fine without it. In a later chapter of *Saint Maybe,* Ian thinks at a church service that: "Coming here had saved him, he knew. Without the Church of the Second Chance he would have struggled alone forever, sunk in hopelessness."[1] In "People Who Don't Know the Answers," how does Doug face the difficult things in his life, the things that Ian knows would have sunk him in hopelessness? Which do you think is the wiser position, Doug's or Ian's?

Notes

1. Anne Tyler, *Saint Maybe* (New York: Alfred A. Knopf, 1991), 211.

3

Henry Louis Gates, Jr.

In recent years, controversies at colleges and universities about curricula, literary canons, and cultural studies have spilled over into the general public. For the previous few decades, when theories of interpretation known as structuralism, deconstruction, and post-structuralism gained ascendancy in the academy, many scholars turned away from a wide audience to write and speak in arcane language intelligible only to each other. In doing so, they abandoned the public voice embraced by earlier thinkers, such as Lionel Trilling and Edmund Wilson. The recent upheavals in the academy, though, have spurred some scholars to reassume the role of public intellectual, to speak and write about issues of consequence for a general audience.

Among the most important of these new intellectuals is Henry Louis Gates, Jr., the W. E. B. DuBois Professor of Humanities, chairman of the Afro-American Studies Department, and professor of English at Harvard University. In forums such as newspaper opinion/editorial pieces, articles for journals with large circulations, and now in his memoir, *Colored People* (1994), Gates seeks to communicate his ideas and experiences to a wide range of readers. In doing so, he tries to engage many more people in thought about the issues he discovers and develops in his literary scholarship than he would by writing in what he calls the "difficult jargon" of "high theory" for a narrow audience.[1] Like the work of Cornel West, Edward Said, Allan Bloom, and Stephen Carter, Gates's writing addresses questions of significance both for the academy and for society-at-large. These questions range from "What do we teach in freshman English classes?" to "How do we 'forge a new, and vital, common American culture in the twenty-first century'?"[2]

Gates's early academic writings do not suggest the public scope his work takes today. His first books, *Figures in Black: Words, Signs, and the "Racial" Self* (1987) and *The Signifying Monkey: A Theory of Afro-American Literary Criticism* (1988), reflect his early interest and training in literary "high theory." Reflecting the kind of work Gates did as an undergraduate at Yale, a Ph.D. student at Cambridge University in England, and then as assistant professor at Yale, these books show how "high theory" may illumine African and African American stories and texts. Gates's achievement in these books was to bring previously ignored or unknown writing into the mainstream of literary criticism.

After he left Yale in 1985 to go first to Cornell, then to Duke, and finally to Harvard, Gates's work moved in new directions. While his interest in lost or ignored African American texts has continued to propel him, he has adopted a more accessible style in which to write about them and the cultural issues his work raises.[3] Commenting on this change in style, Gates has said: "In the recent past, using a denser, much more difficult language was thought somehow to justify what we [scholars in the humanities] do more readily than using an accessible kind of language. I think it's a mistake...."[4]

Gates's change in style is readily apparent in his articles for periodicals and in his memoir, *Colored People*. It also characterizes his most recent scholarly book, *Loose Canons: Notes on the Culture Wars* (1992), which he begins by stating the underlying premise of his new work: "Ours is a late–twentieth-century world profoundly fissured by nationality, ethnicity, race, class, and gender. And the only way to transcend those divisions—to forge, for once, a civic culture that respects both differences and commonalities—is through education that seeks to comprehend the diversity of human culture. Beyond the hype and the high-flown rhetoric is a pretty homely truth: There is no tolerance without respect—and no respect without knowledge."[5] The voice Gates uses here, one addressed to educated but general readers, allows him to communicate to a wide audience his concern for the common good and his conviction that education can effect change in society.

Ironically, the book Gates has written with the largest potential readership, *Colored People*, he addresses specifically to his two daughters, Maggie and Liza. In its preface, Gates offers a letter to his daughters, explaining why he has chosen to write his memoirs for them. They have been puzzled and surprised, he says, by his accounts of the civil rights movement; they are shocked, for instance, to learn that their father would not have been allowed to stay at a motel in his hometown in West Virginia prior to that movement. And they are discomfited by their father's greeting strangers, who are fellow blacks, on the street. Gates's realization that his daughters knew nothing of what he calls the "sepia tones" of his childhood in the 1950s brings him to write *Colored People*.

In the book, he says, he hopes to evoke for them "a colored world of the fifties, a Negro world of the early sixties, and the advent of a black world of the later sixties" so that they will understand how much American society has changed and why, perhaps surprisingly for many of his other readers, he finds that change "a source both of gladness and of regret."[6] For, he says, "I'm divided. I want to be black, to know black, to luxuriate in whatever I might be calling blackness at any particular time—but to do so in order to come out the other side, to experience a humanity that is neither colorless nor reducible to color."[7] For these reasons, he tells his daughters his story of his childhood in Piedmont, West Virginia, "a story of a village, a family, and its friends."[8]

A crucial part of Gates's story is his account of his religious experiences and beliefs. In a section of the book he calls "Saved," he tells how he was faced at a young age with both a personal crisis—the operations necessary to repair his damaged hip—and a public crisis—the race riots in Los Angeles, Detroit, and other large American cities. Gates found in conversations with priests and in the books they gave him the intellectual rigor he looked for to face the daunting questions of good and evil these crises raised. Father Smith, a local Episcopal priest who visited the fouteen-year-old Gates frequently during his six-month hospital stay, showed the boy a way to move beyond what had begun to seem the rigid "do's and don't's" of his childhood religious experience. The priest encouraged him to find instead an intellectually challenging and vigorous religious belief. Gates's subsequent summer stays at an Episcopal church camp offered him both that intellectual satisfaction and a sense of shared community that could transcend the evils of the racism that spawned the riots of the 1960s.

At the camp, too, a priest gave Gates a copy of James Baldwin's *Notes of a Native Son,* and so introduced him to the writer who, Gates has said, has become his "silent, second text."[9] The integrated world of his church camp gave Gates an entree to the African American literature that would eventually become his life's work. Ironically, though, joining an integrated church also removed Gates to some extent from his African American heritage, and he experienced this as a loss. Episcopalian hymns, for instance, are no match in his mind for Miss Toot's gospel songs.

The losses and gains of the religious growth that Gates recounts in "Saved" mirror the losses and gains he experienced after he left Piedmont to join the integrated world of prestigious British and American universities. Gates's memoir ends with his matriculation at Yale; but the story of his intellectual maturation in "Saved" suggests that his rigorous thinking about religious belief continues even as he joins an increasingly influential group of academics in charting a new public role for intellectuals in America.

Paula J. Carlson

Notes

1. Henry Louis Gates, Jr., *Loose Canons: Notes on the Culture Wars* (Oxford: Oxford University Press, 1992), xiii.

2. *Loose Canons: Notes on the Culture Wars*, xvii. On the importance of African Americans among the new public intellectuals, see Robert S. Boynton, "The New Intellectuals," *Atlantic Monthly* (March 1995): 53-70.

3. Gates's work on African American texts includes editing the multi-volume *Schomburg Library of Nineteenth-Century Black Women Writers* (Oxford: Oxford University Press, 1988) and co-editing *The Norton Anthology of Afro-American Literature* (New York: Norton, 1990).

4. Henry Louis Gates, Jr., quoted by Sam Haselby in "Muscular Humanism: An Interview with Henry Louis Gates, Jr.," *Hungry Mind Review*, no. 31 (1994): 33.

5. *Loose Canons: Notes on the Culture Wars*, xv.

6. Henry Louis Gates, Jr., *Colored People: A Memoir* (New York: Alfred A. Knopf, 1994): xvi.

7. *Colored People: A Memoir*, xv.

8. *Colored People: A Memoir*, xvi.

9. Gates, as quoted in "Muscular Humanism," 64.

Saved

Change of Life

Though I didn't realize it at the time, probably the biggest reason I joined the church was Mama. Mama, who knew so well how life could kill the thing that made you laugh, who remembered at every funeral what a person had hoped to be, not what he had become, seemed to be dying herself, before my eyes.

It came with menopause, and that's how we talked about it. Because we never had the vocabulary to talk about what it turned out to be, a depressive disorder that never quite left her. In fact, she was never the same again, but of course permanence is something you recognize afterward. I can say that a veil passed over her life, dimming her radiance, and then never quite lifted away.

I was twelve and she was forty-six when it started, and it was beyond my comprehension. I only knew that something had eclipsed the woman who gave birth to me and raised me, and that nothing I could do seemed to restore things. I was powerless, and so was she. Mama's "change" was the great crisis in my life, the crossroads of my childhood. I was devastated.

It was when Mama got sick that I began to withdraw from other kids. She'd talk about dying for hours. She told me to prepare for her death. She'd tell me she was in a lot of pain. And then she would cry. No amount of love could help. I'm very sick, she would say, and I believe I'm going to die. You'll live with your father, and things will be OK. But it is important that you prepare yourself, she repeated.

I noticed smaller changes. Mama, the fearless one, suddenly became afraid of dogs. She started to alter physically, as well. Mama used to do exercises devoutly and weighed a trim ninety-eight pounds. At about this time, though, she gained fifty or sixty pounds. Then the clutter in our home started, because she would buy canned goods obsessively, as if to stock a bomb shelter we didn't have. She began to buy cloth too, bolts of material for some future occasion. Before long, there were galvanized garbage cans filled with bolts of cloth. A sense of need, born of a childhood of scarcity, now came upon her, spurring a pack rat's notion of providence—a contained panic about running short. Running out. Going without. Needing and not having. Even as the house became cluttered with her acquisitions, she became obsessed with cleanliness, spending a good part of each day vacuuming. Vacuuming and dusting. I liked trying to help her, and would cook, and clean, and even iron sometimes. I would read the pamphlets that started appearing all over our house, with titles such as "The Phases of Eve" and "The Change of Life," so that I might get a handle on this crazy, evil thing that had entered our lives.

I could not break the spell, no matter how ardently I labored. The depression only deepened that year, and I watched her grow sadder every day.

The night they took her away to the hospital, she hugged me as if that was the end. I cried until I fell asleep, afraid that she would die, afraid that I was responsible. And if I was, as I suspected, responsible, I had a good idea how.

You see, I had developed all sorts of rituals. I would, for instance, always walk around the kitchen table only from right to left, never the other way around. I would approach a chair from its left side, not the right. Mama had hung a beautiful oak crucifix in the hall that connected our bedrooms and the toilet, and I would nod my head as I passed it, just as I had seen my father do at the Episcopal funeral of his father. I got into and out of the same side of bed, slept on the same side, and I held the telephone with the same hand to the same ear. But most of all, as if my life depended on it, I crossed my legs right calf over left, and never, ever, the other way around.

Until one Sunday. For a reason that seemed compelling at the time, probably out of anger or spite, I decided that day to cross my legs in reverse. It was a dare, an act of defiance, a deliberate tempting of fate. And it took place just after Sunday supper, at about 1:00 P.M. Mama had not felt like getting dressed that day. She was having "hot flashes," as she'd started to call them, and felt "disconnected," disembodied from herself. She was going to die, she said to me, over and over and over that day. She'd had one "spell" in the middle of a funeral, just a couple of Sundays before. I wasn't there, but I heard that my aunts Helen and Hazel had taken her out of the church to Hazel's house, where the post-funeral meal was being served. Talking crazy talk, was the way Daddy still describes it. Out of her head.

And on this afternoon, the sense of illness lay so heavy you could have gathered it in your hands like snow and rounded it into balls to throw. We all waited for something terrible to happen. And then it was Mama who told me, through her tears, that she had to go to the hospital, that she didn't know when she would be coming back, and that if she shouldn't come back, I must never forget that she loved me.

She didn't die. After her hospitalization of four or five days she started taking a lot of pills prescribed by the doctors, which accumulated like everything else. She had weathered acute depression, but despite real improvement, she did not emerge healthy and whole, as I had dared to hope. Her phobias would evolve in unpredictable ways. In later years, she developed a fear that objects resting on a table or a countertop would fall off the edge. She would go around the house pushing objects farther back from perilous edges. It puzzled and vexed me: I'd point out, in a reasoning tone, that it would take an earthquake to produce the results she feared. But Mama felt her life had been shaken by just such an earthquake; she knew how easy it was to fall off the edge.

As did I in my own way. My metaphor was an untethered craft, battered by frigid waters, too far out for me to bring back to shore.

But Mama wasn't the only one to change. I could never shake the idea that if only I hadn't dared fate to punish me, by crossing my legs the wrong way around, Mama wouldn't have become sick and gone to the hospital. It was a sense of guilt so enormous that I couldn't talk about it. Except to Jesus. That Sunday when Mama went away, I started to atone. I prayed all day, all evening, and the next day: if God would just let Mama not die, as she was convinced she was going to do, I would give my life to Christ and join the church.

After enough time had passed to show that the Lord had kept His side of the covenant, it fell to me to fulfill mine. When I announced my intention to join the church, Daddy thought I'd taken leave of my senses. Mama, quietly wrestling with her own devils, was more tolerant, of course, but even I saw that she hoped I would outgrow it. If you go into this thing, Daddy said quietly, scarcely able to believe his ears, don't do it halfway. And don't be a quitter. Nobody likes a quitter.

Nobody my age had joined the church in years, at least not the Methodist church. I had been thinking about doing it for several months, since I had turned twelve. It was 1962. Each time in the service when Reverend Monroe would invite all who wished to make Jesus their personal Savior to come forward and enter the circle, I had been tempted to go. But I waited until a Sunday afternoon service in Keyser. Reverend Mon-roe had two churches, you see; he preached at Walden in Piedmont, but his primary pulpit was in Keyser, and he'd shuttle from one to the other, preaching in one and then the other, each Sunday.

I sat there throughout the service, nervous and tense. My stomach was doing flip-flops. I thought he'd never read the invitation; I thought he'd never stop that boring sermon.

When finally he did, I found myself rising mechanically, stumbling out

of the pew, wandering to the front of the church, standing right in front of
Ralph Edell Mon-roe, and wondering what would happen next. Nobody
quite knew what to do. It had been so long since anyone joined the church
that no one could remember what came next. Mon-roe stumbled through
the book of rites until he found the right page, and then he asked me the
prescribed questions.

> Do you here, in the presence of God and of this congregation, renew the
> solemn promise contained in the Baptismal Covenant, ratifying and confirm-
> ing the same, and acknowledging yourselves bound faithfully to observe and
> keep the covenant, and all things contained therein?
>
> Have you saving faith in the Lord Jesus Christ?
>
> Do you entertain friendly feelings towards all the members of the Church?
>
> Do you believe in the doctrines of the Holy Scriptures as set forth in the arti-
> cles of religion of the Methodist Church?
>
> Will you cheerfully be governed by the Discipline of the Methodist Church,
> hold sacred the ordinances of God, and endeavor, as much as in you lies, to
> promote the welfare of your brethren, and the advancement of the Redeemer's
> kingdom?
>
> Will you contribute of your earthly substance according to your ability, to the
> support of the Gospel, Church, and poor, and the various benevolent enter-
> prises of the Church?

Yes, yes, and yes! I answered as forcefully as I could, and the reverend
proclaimed the reception address:

> We welcome you to the communion of the Church of God; and in testimony
> of your Christian affection and the cordiality with which we receive you, I
> hereby extend to you the right hand of our fellowship; and may God grant
> that you may be a faithful and useful member of the Church militant till you
> are called to the fellowship of the Church triumphant, which is without fault
> before the presence of God.

Then, departing from the text, he invited everyone in the church—all of
them older women—to march single file to the front and welcome me into
the fold. God bless you, Skippy, each one said, shaking my hand warmly, or
hugging me, or running her hand over my forehead or across my head. That
part was so beautiful that I couldn't help but cry. I stood there crying and
shaking hands, until everyone had passed by. Then I sat down again.

The first thing I did after joining the church was to go down to the Five
and Ten Cent Store, to the school-supply section, where they stocked the

boxes of twelve, twenty-four, and sixty-four Crayola crayons. There I discreetly placed $1.18, in change, down between the neatly stacked cartons. I had stolen a box of crayons when I was six, and wanted to atone for my sin by repaying the store, with interest, for my crime.

I began to cook most of the evening meals for the family. When Mama felt like doing the cooking, I would bake: cakes and corn pudding. I still remember the two Betty Crocker cookbooks she had. They were the same shade of green as the *Webster's Dictionary* that Daddy used for doing the crossword puzzles every day. I loved to cook *with* Mama, just to be near her, to be talking with her. But I was constantly frustrated that we never had all the ingredients a recipe would call for, so I couldn't ever get it exactly right. What is oregano? I'd ask my mother, unsure how to pronounce it. And what in the world was cumin? I'd spend hours searching for a recipe that called only for ingredients that Mama stocked. They were few and far between. Furthermore, Betty didn't season with bacon drippings or ham hocks, and she didn't cook the vegetables long enough to suit us.

For the next two years, I didn't play cards, I didn't go to dances, I didn't listen to rock and roll; I didn't gamble or swear, as my classmates did. I didn't even lust in my heart—except once or twice for Brenda. I went to church, and read the Bible, and spent a lot of time thinking about questions that it turned out Miss Sarah and even Reverend Mon-roe weren't prepared to answer for me.

I enjoyed my time alone: I had to, since I hardly went anywhere during these two years, except for school and church. It gave me distance from Daddy and Rocky, neither of whom seemed to be crazy about the person I was becoming. It gave me space to think about Mama's change and a way to use my prayers to help her. It gave me a way to stop thinking so much about nuclear war. For the world now seemed a dangerous place, and the Cuban missile crisis of 1962 provided bleak confirmation. We all went to bed one night thinking that we were going to die in some terrible, horrible, nasty way. I prayed and prayed until I fell asleep. Ain't no use worrying about bomb shelters, Daddy had said. It won't help much. I just wanted to be at home when it happened, with Mama and Daddy and Rocky. I was worried that Daddy might not get to Heaven, as much as he cussed and played cards. The church would help with my worries about Vietnam, where my cousin Jay had been sent. His mother, Aunt Marguerite, was so upset she stopped reading the papers.

Larger things began to worry me, now. After I became a Christian and was saved, I was terrified that an angel would show up in my room, bearing some ominous message from God, or that such a message would appear in the form of Writing on the Wall. Miss Sarah would talk of that all the time.

I agonized constantly that a bad-news message from God would delineate my role in life, my obligations to God and to our people. That was one of the reasons I was afraid of the dark. I was terrified of the Visitation that would make me an agent of salvation. More concretely, I feared that one day I'd open my mouth and somebody else's voice would come out, as the Spirit possessed me to do its bidding.

I didn't want it to be like that. I didn't want to be an automaton controlled by heavenly remote. What I did feel was that God spoke His will to my heart if I asked what I should do in a given situation. I still ask, and, generally, I still hear. Sooner or later.

In those days, I spent long hours wondering about, and worrying about, God, Jesus, being born again, eternal life, Hell, the Devil, why bad things happen to good people, why good things happen to bad people, and what is right and what wrong.

In the end, as I say, joining the church gave me a space of my own, and I found solace in that solitude, long after I realized that the time had come to part ways with our small white wooden church.

Eternity

A man is talking to the Lord, trying to fathom His infinitude. "Lord," he asks, "what's a million years to you?" "A million years is a second to me," the Lord explains. "And a million dollars?" A penny, the Lord replies. "Lord," the man proceeds to ask, emboldened, "would you give me a million dollars?" "Sure," the Lord replies. "Just a second."

When I was in the church, between the ages of twelve and fourteen, staying at home and praying a lot, I used to try to imagine how long eternity could be. "A thousand years is like the blink of an eye to the Lord," Miss Sarah Russell would say. One day, our eighth-grade science teacher, Mr. McGoye, told us that to begin to imagine the length of eternity, we should think of a hummingbird. This hummingbird lands upon a huge stone once every five hundred years. The stone is five hundred miles high, five hundred miles wide, and five hundred miles thick. And once every five hundred years, this tiny little hummingbird lands on this rock and sharpens its beak. The length of time it takes the hummingbird to file down that huge stone to the size of a pebble is the equivalent of *one second* of eternity. He stopped the entire class dead with that one. Especially me. (Only later, when I encountered a similar passage in Joyce's *A Portrait of the Artist as a Young Man*, did I realize that such imagery enjoyed considerable currency.)

Sitting up in Heaven with Miss Sarah and Reverend Mon-roe for *that* many years, listening to Mr. Lynn Allen and Mr. Doug Twyman argue about whose turn it was to say the morning prayer, was about as appealing as getting a typhoid shot in your behind every day. Who ever thought eternity was a good idea in the first place?

I suppose the shake-up of my spiritual creed was hastened by my realization that I was religious in part because I was scared, scared of Jesus coming back to earth and sending me to Hell, scared of being liquidated or vaporized in a nuclear holocaust, scared of what was happening to my mother— scared, in all likelihood, of life itself.

Uncle Harry, that is, the Reverend Harry A. Coleman, talked me into going to church camp at the end of the summer of my thirteenth year. He and a buddy he'd studied with at Boston University Seminary in the fifties decided to hold a Methodist retreat for teenagers somewhere "up in the country," which means somewhere in Grant or Hardy county, near Williamsport, where Big Mom was born. What I most remember about that camp was sitting by the big campfire and staring longingly into the dark-brown eyes of Eileen Redman, hoping that by some act of the Good Lord Himself this angel of beauty would fall in love with me while we all sang "Kumbaya."

Also memorable that August was a touch football game during which I noticed a sharp pain in my knee. I decided it would be best to retire from the field.

The pain would not go away. I tried elastic wraps and liniment, Deep Heat and Aspercreme, exercising it and resting it, and still it would not go away. I went to see one Dr. Reeves, and he said I had pulled a muscle. I went to see his brother, the other Dr. Reeves, and he said I had torn a ligament. The first Dr. Reeves gave me a cane to use. The second gave me a set of crutches. I was still on them in September when school started. Mr. McGoye, who made beautiful colored chalk drawings of the inside of flora and fauna on the blackboard, started calling me Gimp and Gold Brick.

I was having lunch one day, just across from the high school, at the only sandwich shop over in the Orchard. It had been segregated, until Mrs. Wattie came to town. She was the typing teacher, whom everyone called Mrs. Watusi behind her back. She was young, and she was pretty, but most of all, she was black. Mr. Staggers, the principal, had told the manager of that shop that if Dolores Wattie couldn't eat there, no teacher would eat there, and the place integrated, just like that.

I sat at a table all by myself, since most of the kids went home for lunch. Eating out was not a big concept in Piedmont. They don't want us in there anyway, colored people would say as they drove down the highway, passing restaurants, pulling over at rest stops to munch on picnic lunches in their cars. (One shivery fear possessed us: we believed that if we went to eat where we weren't wanted, they'd spit in our food before serving it.)

But there I was in the freshly integrated sandwich shop, a living, munching symbol of the new dispensation. Martin Luther King come to Piedmont.

I looked over to watch Mrs. Houchins, the gym teacher, who had a beautiful aquiline nose and a charming gap between her front teeth. She was perky and alert and had a large, warm laugh. She also wore short skirts and tight blouses, so she was the favorite work of art among the ninth-grade boys. I watched her crumble a packet of crackers while it was still wrapped in cellophane, then dump the contents into her bowl of chili. It was such a neat trick that I thought how very clever she was. I watched her eat that bowl of chili, and she let me watch her, rolling her spoon over her lips as if that chili were her last meal and my eyes were her final testament.

I limped happily back toward school. We were having an assembly at one o'clock, and I wanted to get a good seat. I was doing fine until I passed the swimming pool.

Three or four feet from the swimming pool's double doors, I ran into a wall of pain. It seemed to rise up out of the earth, surrounding me on all sides. I was inside that pain, and it was inside me. I couldn't move outside the pain, I couldn't shake it off. It wasn't like when you hit your funny bone hard and think you'll lose your mind for a minute. And it wasn't like bumping your head on an overhang, or twisting your ankle, or stubbing your toe. It wasn't *like* anything. This kind of pain lived in its own dimension, and I could hardly see because of it. To move was only to make it worse, left or right, up or down. I was frozen in midstep.

Petie Ross was the first to come by. Petie was black as slate, twice my size, and mean as the day was long. I was as frightened of him as everybody else was. But even Petie sensed that this was no time to play. He grabbed another boy and told me to use the two of them like crutches, and they would carry me to school. On the count of three they lifted. My scream scared even Petie. He sent for the principal. And for Petie Ross to call for Mr. Staggers was like Al Capone summoning Eliot Ness. I *knew* I must be sick. It seemed to take an hour to get me into the back seat of the taxi that had been called. I screamed again when it crossed the tracks, each bump like a hammer drilling deep inside me. I was very afraid.

"It's a torn ligament in your knee," the surgeon said, ignoring completely the fact that my hip joint was disconnected. (One of the signs of what I had—a "slipped epithesis"—is intense knee pain, I later learned.) So he scheduled me for a walking cast.

I was wheeled into surgery and placed on the operating table, where the surgeon proceeded to wrap my leg with wet plaster strips that would dry into a hard cast, like white concrete. As he worked, he asked questions about my schoolwork, I guess to make the time pass.

"Boy," he said, "I understand you want to be a doctor."

"Yessir." You always said "sir" to white people—unless you were trying to make a statement.

Had I taken a lot of science courses? he wanted to know.

I said, "Yessir. I enjoy science."

"Are you good at it?"

"Yessir, I believe so."

He said, "Tell me, who was the father of sterilization?"

"Joseph Lister."

Then he asked who discovered penicillin.

Alexander Fleming, I answered.

And what about DNA?

Watson and Crick.

The interview went on like this. I thought my answers might get me a pat on the head. Actually, they just confirmed a medical judgment he'd come to.

That's why he stood me on my feet and insisted that I walk. But with the best intentions in the world, there are some things you can't do when your ball and socket are completely separated. So it's not surprising that the joint sheared and I fell on the floor in agony. I wasn't a doctor, but even I figured out something wasn't right.

The doctor shook his head and walked over to my mother, who was waiting in the corridor. "Pauline," he said, his voice kindly but amused, "there's not a thing wrong with that child. The problem's psychosomatic. Because I know the type, and the thing is, your son's an overachiever."

Now, there's an interesting history to that term, and what it meant in Piedmont in 1964 wasn't what it usually means today. Back then, "over-achiever" designated a sort of pathology: the dire consequence of overstraining your natural capacity. A colored kid who thought he could be a doctor—just for instance—was headed for a breakdown.

What made the pain abate was my mother's reaction. You have to understand that I'd never, ever heard my mother talk back to a white person before. And doctors, well, doctors were sacred, and their word was scripture.

Not this time. After the doctor said his piece, Pauline Gates stared at him for a moment and announced her decision. "Get his clothes, pack his bags—we're going to the University Medical Center." That was sixty miles away, in Morgantown.

Which wasn't great news as far as I was concerned. The one thing I knew was that they only moved you to the University Medical Center when you were going to die. I was inconsolable.

But it turned out Mama was right. And I wasn't going to die. I had three operations in the course of that year. After the first, in which the joint was pinned together with a metal pin, I walked on crutches for six weeks and began to lose even more weight than I'd lost in the hospital. By the time I got back to school, I was four or five weeks behind. This was not a major problem, except in geometry. I was scared about geometry anyway; I was taking it with the juniors and seniors, and wasn't sure how smart I really was. Low expectations, stay quiet, observe everything. The problem was that I couldn't figure out how $a^2 + b^2$ could *always* equal c^2, until the day when I realized that the letters referred to the sides of a right triangle and c was the hypotenuse. Once I figured that out, learning geometry became one of the most pleasurable experiences of my educational life. I loved its order and logic; I loved making a formal proof. I loved learning its axioms and lemmas. I loved coming to visualize three-dimensional structures on a flat plane. By the time we got to the unit about 5-12-13 triangles, the doctors had decided that the steel pins they had inserted in my hip had failed. I would need a second operation to remove the pins, and then a third operation in June.

Following the last procedure, a "cup arthroplasty"—a metal ball on the hip—I was confined to bed for six weeks, immobilized by a complex system of weights and pulleys, unable to attend to even the simplest of bodily movements or functions. It was six weeks of bondage—and bedpans. It was also when I had my first glimpse of eternity.

Eternity is a fourteen-year-old strapped down to a bed, held rigidly in place by traction and a system of pulleys and weights, unable to move to the left or to the right, to lift up his body beyond forty-five degrees, unable to turn over, unable to use the bathroom ... for six weeks. Forty-two long, hot days. One thousand and eight hours. In my mind, that little hummingbird flew back and forth, sharpening its beak on the promontory.

Each day for six weeks, my mother would walk up the big hill in front of the hospital and sit with me from nine to nine, from the time they allowed her in until the time they sent her home. I spent my time quarreling with her. She had rented a small room—which we could ill afford—in a motel that was reserved for the families of patients, just down the hill from the medical center.

Every day, in the middle of the latest quarrel, I'd insist that she go back to Piedmont—or she would insist that she was going back to Piedmont. I think we both came to realize that this was a sort of ritual. I didn't like being a patient, and stoicism wasn't my strong suit. We'd argue about everything and anything—even about what time of day it was—but the arguments kept me from thinking about that traction system. And maybe they helped her escape her own darkening obsessions.

I learned to play chess there; the doctors would come and play with me, especially a surgeon from the Philippines, a brown-skinned man, with dark, wavy hair. He'd drop by, we'd make two or three moves, he'd disappear on his rounds, then he'd return just as abruptly as he'd left. I enjoyed his company, enjoyed the fact that I could give him a run for his money, at least on the chessboard.

I had to learn to walk again, after relearning how to use all the atrophied muscles in my right leg. One day, the chief surgeon asked me to move my leg, using a system of pulleys that had been installed the previous day. After six weeks of nonmovement, to lift my leg even with the pulley was agonizing. He shook his head and said that it didn't look good for an early release for me, until I could retrain those muscles.

I was horrified. I had to get out of that bed. Using a bedpan, and needing an orderly to clean your body afterward, is not much fun. (The orderlies, for their part, were sensitive to my embarrassment and vulnerability. One of them happened to mention to me one day that toilet paper had been invented in 1859. It has become a crucial date for me: 1859. B.T.P. and A.T.P: Before Toilet Paper and After Toilet Paper. It made me wonder about people's toilet habits before 1859. What was Frederick Douglass up to when he used the bathroom in 1842, just before his big speech? Or Plato? Or Shakespeare? Or Shaka Zulu?)

Finally, that day came when the surgeon challenged me to retrain my leg muscles. Almost as soon as he and the interns and the resident had left my room, I decided to try my leg muscles once more. It hurt like hell. I set my jaw and pulled again, slowly this time, ever so slowly but gently and steadily, until my knee bent at a forty-five-degree angle as it was supposed to do. It hurt so much that I asked Mama to leave. I did it again, even more slowly, then again. And again. I'd rest a bit, massage myself, and do it again. By the time the surgeon made his rounds the next day, I could pull up that leg as easily as I wanted to. Hey, Doc, I said, look at this! What's next?

I liked my medical team, mostly because they answered my questions. They talked with me. Fear is everywhere in a hospital. All those hours of the night and day, waiting for a surgeon to come by, then getting five minutes, maximum, to allay your concerns, and spending the next twenty-three hours and fifty-five minutes scared and anxious.

But in some ways the most important words I received were not medical but religious. While I was in the medical center, a new Episcopal priest in Keyser would drive the two hours or so it took to see me in Morgantown. Father Smith had fat jowls and a red face. I liked his robust laugh and his fat, jelly-shaking sides. The flesh of his neck hung around the edge of his collar like dough for a pie crust that hasn't yet been trimmed. The word he bore was that I could drink, smoke, curse, and still be a good Episcopalian. I could even date girls. Now, *that* part was beginning to appeal to me. In fact, the whole thing appealed to me. I wanted to have a spiritual life without being imprisoned by it. I wanted to be a religious person, but I no longer wanted to be a member of Walden Methodist, with its oppressive literalisms.

By this time, the worst of Mama's depression appeared to be over, though it would return in a few years. Her regimen of hormones and other medications had restored her to a reasonable semblance of normality. The woman who stood up to the doctor in the Keyser hospital and who watched over my recuperation at the medical center was the mother I was afraid I had lost. And her own measure of recovery helped to free me from my commitment to the restrictive fundamentalism that I had so desperately embraced.

What happened during my hospital stay sealed my decision, but it is clear to me that my disenchantment had been brewing for a while. Part of it was about my growing alienation from my younger Coleman uncles. The more I succeeded in school, the more I rejected their advice, the more bitterly we argued, the quieter they got around me, at least about my successes—though they got louder about my racial politics and my growing discomfort with the Vietnam war. I had been tiring of Miss Sarah, Reverend Mon-roe, and the Methodist church. It was as if I had outgrown a good pair of trousers, my favorite trousers, and had no others to put on. I wanted to learn how to be a free Negro and to be a man, how to be in the world and with God, how to question values and tradition without being kicked out of the fold, how to value community and order, family and the group, yet not have to suppress my uncertainties, doubts, ambivalences in order to be accepted. Soon church for me was only the music, and only Miss Toot's gospel choir at that.

Father Smith seemed to understand all this. He gave me books to read— all kinds of books. Prayer books and catechisms, philosophical and historical works about the church, books like *The Secular City* and *The Other America. Are You Running With Me, Jesus?* blew me away because this priest was talking to God just like He was one of the boys. Anything even remotely like this would have been heresy to Miss Sarah. She would have gotten down on her knees and prayed to Jesus to help me see the light. God became for me a spirit or force that guides, rather than Rex Ingram in *The Green Pastures.*

Father Smith treated me as an equal in conversation; and he didn't think an awakening skepticism was inconsistent with an adolescent's underlying faith. He seemed to offer an intellectual framework to go with my spirituality.

Plus, I didn't see why God should mind if I saw the occasional movie, listened to popular music, or took a turn, however ungainly, on the dance floor. My brother used to claim that I checked into the hospital with a Bible in one hand and a cross in the other, then checked out with a deck of cards and a saxophone.

Eventually, I was released from that bed of Procrustes. For the next six months, I walked on crutches; then I used a cane. Gradually, a cane became part of my identity, as did orthopedic shoes with a lift in the right heel. I regarded them with a feeling of despair. Having been freed from the corrective shoes of my boyhood, I was consigned to them again. Finding shoes that did what they were supposed to do and still looked half decent was a difficult business. Each year, it seemed, I needed more of a lift to balance myself, as the metal ball on my hip migrated farther north. In time, I myself would follow suit.

Living Under Grace

It was at Peterkin, an Episcopal church camp in West Virginia that I attended that summer—the summer of 1965—and the two summers following, that I was given an opportunity to explore the contours of my new faith, and the world beyond Piedmont.

Spending two weeks at Peterkin, made possible by a scholarship, was like stepping into a dream world. It was populated by well over a hundred seemingly self-confident, generous-spirited teenagers, their ages ranging from fifteen to eighteen; they were rebellious, worldly, questioning, cosmopolitan, articulate, bold, and smart. I learned so much at that camp, I don't even know where to begin.

Following a regular regime of breakfast, morning prayers in the chapel, cleanup, seminars, then lunch, we'd sit for long hours in the afternoon, playing hands of bridge, which I was learning as I went along. We'd play on the front porch of the main house, which used to be an elegant hunting lodge, complete with a huge stone fireplace. I had beginner's luck: a couple of small slams, a grand slam, hands with lots of points. We'd play, the four of us—Tandy Tully and her boyfriend, Peter Roberts, Andrea Strader and I—all afternoon sometimes, watching the other campers come and go, and we'd talk about this and that and everything, books and ideas, people and concepts. The war in Vietnam. Smoking. The existence of God.

Andrea was smart and well-read, intuitive and analytical. She was also beautiful, cocoa-colored, with a wide plum-purple mouth that tasted delicious. It was Andrea who told me early on that I should go to prep school, and then to the Ivy League. (What's a prep school? I asked her.) That I should travel and read this and that. She was petite and elegant, and she sang like an angel. Every night we'd have a campfire, and every night I'd sit next to her, trying to learn the words of the traditional gospel songs and the camp songs, listening to my past and future through Andrea's lovely voice. She had large black eyes and long, straightened hair that was soft to the touch. I couldn't believe that she even existed or that she would want to be with me.

The third black camper at Peterkin was Eddie James—Edward Lawrence James, The Third, thank you very much. Eddie was rich. His grandfather had founded a produce business in Charleston at the turn of the century, and it had prospered. Everybody in Charleston knew and respected the Jameses, he let us know. All the Democratic politicians kissed Mr. James II's black behind. Money can't erase color, Andrea would explain to me, but sometimes it can help you blend a bit better. The Jameses were proof of that. Eddie was dating a white girl at camp, which was giving the director, Mary Jo Fitts, fits. She chain-smoked so much that her teeth looked like yellow fangs, and her personality matched her teeth.

Sex was everywhere at Peterkin—everywhere but in my bed. Maybe it could have been there, but I didn't know it, and I didn't know how to put it there. I was fond of making all sorts of lofty pronouncements, like: I'm naturally high, or I'll wait to do it until I get married. I was the walking, talking equivalent of those wall plaques that you can buy in Woolworth's that attest to such sentiments as "M Is for the Many Things She Gave Me" or "Lord, Help Us to Accept the Things We Cannot Change." I wonder how people could stand me. But I was being honest, in the same way that people who collect paintings on black velvet are being honest. I thought I was thinking the right things, remaining pure of heart. I was terribly earnest: the Pentheus of Peterkin. Meantime, everybody else was getting down with somebody or other. You could feel the sexual energy flowing. There was a charge in the air.

A month shy of my fifteenth birthday, I felt I had died and gone to Heaven. I was living in a kingdom, one of the princes. We drank ideas and ate controversy. Is God dead? we asked. Can you love two people at the same time? I feasted on the idea of learning about the world and being a citizen of it.

And yet my sense of this citizenship would be jeopardized not long after I arrived. After a solid week of complete isolation, a deliveryman bringing milk and bread to the camp told the head counselor that "all hell has broken loose in Los Angeles" and the "colored people have gone crazy." He handed him a Sunday paper, which screamed the news about Negroes rioting in some place called Watts. Andrea had overheard and was the one to tell me. Your soul brothers have gone totally crazy, she said. Rioting and shit. I stared at the headline: NEGROES RIOT IN WATTS. We were all trying to understand what was really happening, forced to judge from one screaming headline.

I was bewildered. I didn't understand what a riot was. Were colored people being killed by white people, or were they killing white people? Watching myself being watched by all the white campers, I experienced that strange combination of power and powerlessness that you feel when the actions of another black person affect your own life, simply because you both are black. I realized that the actions of people I did not know had become my responsibility as surely as if the black folk in Watts had been my relatives in Piedmont, just twenty or so miles away.

Sensing my mixture of pride and discomfiture, a priest handed me a book later that day. From the cover, the wide-spaced eyes of a black man transfixed me. *Notes of a Native Son,* the book was called, by James Baldwin. Was this man the *author,* I wondered, this man with a closely cropped "natural," with brown skin, splayed nostrils, and wide lips, so very Negro, so seemingly comfortable to be so?

From the book's first few sentences, I was caught up thoroughly in the sensibility of another person—a black person. It was the first time I had heard a voice capturing the terrible exhilaration and anxiety of being a person of African descent in this country. The book performed for me the Adamic function of naming the complex racial dynamic of the American cultural imagination. I could not put it down.

It became all the more urgent to deal with the upheaval I had felt when I read that headline.

We were pioneers, people my age, in cross-race relations, able to get to know each other across cultures and classes in a way that was unthinkable in our parents' generation. Honest hatreds, genuine friendships, rivalries bred from contiguity rather than from the imagination. Love and competition. In school, I had been raised with white kids, from first grade. To speak to white people was just to speak. Period. No artificial tones, no hypercorrectness. And yet I have known so many Negroes who were separated from white people by an abyss of fear. Whenever one of my uncles would speak to a white person, his head would bow, his eyes would widen, and the smile he would force on his lips said: I won't hurt you, boss, an' I'm your faithful friend. Just come here and let ole me help you. Laughing much too loud and too long at their jokes, he assumed the same position with his head and his body as when he was telling a lie.

But there, at Peterkin, on that day especially, we were all trying to understand what had just happened and what it might mean for our lives, and to do so with a measure of honesty.

What the news of the riots did for us was to remind everybody in one fell swoop that there was a racial context outside Peterkin that affected relations between white and black Americans; we had suddenly to remember that our roles were scripted by that larger context. We had for a blissful week been functioning outside these stereotypes of each other—functioning as best we could, that is—when all of a sudden the context had come crashing down upon us once again. I hated that newspaper. But we overcame it: with difficulty, with perseverance, we pushed away the racial context and could interact not as allegories but as people. It felt like something of an achievement.

I didn't want to leave. I cried when I had to go ... but then everybody cried. When I got home, my wonderful room full of books and records looked like Cinderella's hovel must have, when she returned from the ball at half-past midnight. My beautiful mountain valley on the banks of the mighty Potomac looked like a dirty, smelly mill town, full of people who cared more about basketball and baseball and eating than anything else. Somehow, between the six weeks of the hospital and the two weeks of Peterkin, some evil blight had stricken my magical kingdom. It made me heartsick, especially the once or twice I was foolhardy enough to try to explain all this to Linda Hoffman or to Johnny DiPilato. There are *lots* of nice church camps, was all that Hoffman said.

It was in 1966, between my first summer at Peterkin and my second, that I gave up the evangelical Methodist Church for good. It happened on the afternoon that Rocky prevailed upon me to flout my renunciation of cinema in favor of Heaven and dragged me down to Searstown at Cumberland to see *A Hard Day's Night*. He had come back from college for the weekend. I had *heard* of the Beatles, but that was about it. When I came out into the light after the movie, which I'd watched with excitement mingled with a certain dread, I took a sidelong glance at the sky. I was as disappointed as I was relieved when no lightning came down to smite me. I almost wanted to see a heavenly show of displeasure.

I joined Father Smith's church in Keyser. I was grateful to him for visiting me in the hospital; and he was a good priest, a village priest. Years later, he would come to my graduation from Yale, even though he had by then left the priesthood. (When he was replaced by Fred Bannerot, a Yalie from Charleston who bragged about being rich, lent me five hundred dollars to pay my expenses at Harvard Summer School—then told half the town about it—I made my final church membership move and joined St. James's in Westernport, closer by, so that Mama, Daddy, and I could walk to church on Sundays and so we could integrate, at last, the last bastion of high-church white men left in our branch of the Potomac Valley.)

Mama and I were confirmed at the same ceremony, at Peterkin. I never saw my father happier at something I did, or prouder. Aunt Beck had stood for me as my godmother. I cried on that day just as I had down at the Methodist church when I joined. Now my father and I started to attend church together.

Ironically, it was becoming an Episcopalian that killed the idea of becoming a minister for me. I had gained the freedom within the church to question just about anything and everything I wanted to, but I found that I did not want to do this from the pulpit. I thought that I needed someone to assuage my doubts, rather than being secure enough to assuage the doubts of others. Besides, I am not fond of uniforms.

The Episcopal Church wasn't without its drawbacks. Some of its songs were lifeless and its sermonic style tended toward the pallid. But it compensated for such failings by its theological freedom, its willingness to let its parishioners range intellectually. Bishop James Pike had even written a book asking *Is God Dead?* without being thrown out of the priesthood or burned at the stake. I liked the prayers; I liked the church's calm and order; I liked the piety of its hymns. I liked the social activism of the young priests of the sixties and seventies, especially that of Father Smith. I loved praying on my knees, right there in church, and taking Communion with real wine, passed in one chalice, hand to hand and mouth to mouth. I loved doing holy days with special services and specific prayers. I loved learning about the history of the holy days, which together spelled out the history of the church itself.

Daddy was delighted when I joined his church, but he didn't want to gloat for fear of jinxing things. Miss Sarah Russell, Sister Holy Ghost, called and pleaded with Mama and Daddy, then shook her head sadly and told me she would pray for me. Uncle Jim said that the Episcopal Church wasn't even a true church, and why didn't I come on across the street with him, Reverend Monk, and Mr. Les, and "become Holiness"? As for me, I felt so much more comfortable in the world, so much more that I belonged in it, than I had before. And I found I didn't miss the Walden Methodist Church much, either, except when I thought about Miss Toot's sublime rendition of "The Prodigal Son" and when I went to funerals.

Guides to Reflection

1. At the opening of "Saved," Gates writes: "Though I didn't realize it at the time, probably the biggest reason I joined the church was Mama. Mama, who knew so well how life could kill the thing that made you laugh, who remembered at every funeral what a person had hoped to be, not what he

had become, seemed to be dying herself, before my eyes" *(Reader, 49)*. Consider Gates's relationship with his mother as he portrays it in "Saved." How does his fear about her illness affect him? How does she influence his religious beliefs?

2. Although Gates "outgrows" the church he joined when he was 12, he vividly portrays in "Saved" the worship service at which he formally joined that church, even including the full text of the questions the minister asked him in the rite. Why do you think Gates included these questions in his memoir? What do his fervent response to them at the service and his subsequent behavior indicate about his emerging religious beliefs?

3. When Gates joins the Episcopalian church, his father is pleased: "Daddy was delighted when I joined his church, but he didn't want to gloat for fear of jinxing things" *(Reader, 65)*. How does this statement reflect the portrayal of Gates's relationship with his father in "Saved"?

4. Gates describes two significant aspects of his time at Peterkin, the Episcopal summer camp he attended as a teenager. First, he recalls the excitement of being in a stimulating and kind intellectual environment: "I felt I had died and gone to Heaven.... We drank ideas and ate controversy.... I feasted on the idea of learning about the world and being a citizen of it" *(Reader, 62)*. And then, he recalls the ability of people at the racially integrated camp to maintain that community despite the racism that fueled hatred and riots: "But we overcame it: with difficulty, with perseverance, we pushed away the racial context and could interact not as allegories but as people. It felt like something of an achievement" *(Reader, 64)*. How do these two elements of summer camp affect Gates's life back in Piedmont? How do the two places—Peterkin and Piedmont—interact in his religious development?

5. While *Colored People* ends with his departure from Piedmont to go to college, Gates at times includes comments in the book about later years. When he discusses prayer in "Saved," for instance, he says: "What I did feel was that God spoke His will to my heart if I asked what I should do in a given situation. I still ask, and, generally, I still hear. Sooner or later" *(Reader, 54)*. Review the places in "Saved" where Gates refers to prayer. How does prayer seem to affect the course of his religious development?

4

Tobias Wolff

In *Matters of Life and Death*, his 1983 collection of new American short stories, Tobias Wolff explained the common characteristics of the authors he chose to bring together: "They write about fear of death, fear of life, the feelings that bring people together and force them apart, the costs of intimacy. They remind us that our house is built on sand. They are, every one of them, interested in what it means to be human."[1]

This evocative description of other writers' work also represents the essential qualities of his own: two collections of short stories, a novella, a memoir *(This Boy's Life,* made into a film in 1993), and, most recently, an account of his experience as a lieutenant in the U. S. Army Special Services in Vietnam *(In Pharaoh's Army,* 1994). This is not to say that his vision of human life as driven by fear, or as a house built on sand, is essentially tragic. He evokes more laughter than tears, more an incredulous "Oh no, not *again!*" rather than King Lear's "Never, never, never, never, never!" And yet, although full of whimsy and surprise, with touches of humor that frequently catch the reader off guard, Wolff ultimately writes about serious business, "matters of life and death."

Often this entails the exploration of a loss of innocence, a crash course in reality. Complacency in particular always has its comeuppance. In "An Episode in the Life of Professor Brooke," for instance, a self-righteous man inadvertently saves his own soul precisely by losing the burden of his virtue: it is a relief in the end to be a sinner like everyone else. In "Sister" the lesson learned is more sad. A young woman realizes finally that there is never to be anyone who will protect her, no one else to reassure her "that everything was going to be all right."[2]

In other stories, it is the status quo itself that receives a challenge, as a character stands up in defiance of the way things are, in refusal of the powers that be. One thinks preeminently of Mary in the title story of the collection *In the Garden of the North American Martyrs.* In a dramatic break with a life spent listening for what it was that other people wanted her to say, and hobbled by the particular caution that weighs down an academic community, she stuns a college audience by "winging it" without prepared notes, by speaking her own mind at last—and in the end, by speaking nothing less than the prophetic word of the Lord.

This is not to say, however, that Wolff has any illusion about the frequency of true heroism. Indeed, many of his stories are about human betrayal, the denial of another person which he counts as "one of the original sins in the world."[3] In "Leviathan" a husband falls asleep when his wife is goaded into telling about the single moment in her life she is most proud of; in "Desert Breakdown, 1968" a young husband and father almost deserts his family for a fantasy of self-fulfillment, and then plans to return to them less as an act of loyalty than in a failure of nerve.

Wolff's fiction is ultimately about the moral life, albeit as it is lived by people who would not be likely to think of their existence in such terms—soldiers, feisty teenagers, men on a hunting trip, estranged couples. Although he acknowledges having learned from a fellow Roman Catholic, Flannery O'Connor, how to move a story toward a moment of choice between good and evil, he also recognizes the great difference between her work and his own: "The choice O'Connor's characters are presented with—or have forced on them—is an irrevocable one, a choice between salvation and damnation." His work, by contrast, is mundane, his characters' gestures more tentative, provisional, and ambiguous. Nor does he court the sublime or clothe his "matters of life and death" in the garments of mystery. Rather, "what saves people has as much to do with the ordinary responsibilities of family, adulthood, and work as it does these violent eruptions from heaven."[4]

What also saves us is the imagination: our ability to conceive of the reality of someone other than ourselves, to transform negative experience into something positive, or even to lie. Wolff is especially interested in youthful liars, partly for autobiographical reasons (as he confesses in *This Boy's Life*), partly because the misrepresentation of reality can also be a way to imagine a world that is more hospitable and more generous to our needs than the one that merely "is." There is also a thin line between making up stories and storytelling, and in many of his works Wolff shows the office of liar and artist to be one and the same, with fiction sometimes telling a deeper truth than fact.

It would be a mistake, however, to think that Wolff views fantasy as an unalloyed good or fiction as necessarily "true." Some lies are destructive, others build community; they can be delusional as well as visionary. In "The Missing Person," for instance, Father Leo suffers from a romantic notion of what his religious vocation means. He has always wanted to imagine himself a missionary laboring nobly within the "polar solitude" of Alaska, a man of God living "a life full of risk among people who needed him and were hungry for what he had to give."[5] In reality, he ends up the chaplain of a dubious convent that by all rights should close down, assisting a con-man fundraiser who has no scruples whatsoever about the truth: "He said that the convent helped orphans, lepers, Navahos, earthquake victims, even pandas and seals. There was no end to what he would do."[6] Leo is eventually deserted by his partner in a Las Vegas casino and pressed into service as a nightwatchman by a needy, manipulative woman desperate for company— even from the likes of him. The situation is ridiculous, not to mention highly irregular for a Roman Catholic priest. And yet in some real sense, Father Leo's bedside vigil in Sandra's hotel room, however comical, ends up being a realization of the missionary vocation he had always wanted. If only for one absurd night in Las Vegas, he has found someone who needs him and the little that he has to give. "'It's all right,' Father Leo said, 'I'm here.'"[7]

"The Rich Brother," which concludes the 1985 collection *Back in the World,* picks up many of the themes found elsewhere in Wolff's fiction, but it works them in a quite distinctive way. One reviewer called it a "small classic about family life in America, what's left of it"[8]; Wolff himself says it is "as close to a fable as I've written."[9] It is, in fact, easy to see the story as an American retelling of the parable of the prodigal son, except that here there is no father to mediate between siblings; there are only "two brothers, Pete and Donald." Wolff heightens the contrast between the two, making the one insufferable in his materialism, the other in his irresponsibility. Pete is the one who rescues, again and again, and Donald is the one who needs to be picked up and cared for, as one disaster follows quickly upon another.

The tension between such different souls finally reaches the breaking point when the gullible Donald "invests" the hundred dollars Pete has given him for food to buy a "share" in a phony Peruvian gold mine. This dumb giveaway of Pete's hard-earned money is the last straw, a sign that Pete is forever stuck with a "prodigal" younger brother who is as much a squanderer as he himself is a man "who has finished his work and settled his debts, done all things meet and due" *(Reader, 85)."* At the end of the story, he seems quite within his rights to drive away and leave his brother to fend for himself. And yet, how is he ever to answer his wife's inevitable question, "Where is he? Where is your brother?" *(Reader, 85).*

For the reader who recognizes that this question is none other than the one God poses to Cain after his slaying of Abel (Genesis 4:9), the story assumes greater significance than a small classic about American family life. It becomes a quasi-biblical probing of tensions as old as Genesis, as venerable as the struggle between Cain and Abel, Esau and Jacob, or Joseph and his brothers. Furthermore, just as Old Testament Scripture shows God's apparently perverse favor of the disadvantaged younger son over the traditionally favored elder, so too "The Rich Brother" raises questions about who is last and who is first, who is wise and who is foolish. Or, as Pete wonders to himself, suddenly insecure about whether or not he has, in fact, won life's game by playing by the sensible rules, "What a joke if there really was a blessing to be had, and the blessing didn't come to the one who deserved it, the one who did all the work, but to the other" *(Reader, 83-84)*.

Pondering this "joke," one recalls the "injustice" of those parables in which the last become first and the first last. Wolff doesn't force a conversion on his version of the prodigal's elder brother. But in the story's final paragraph it is clear that Pete's car is slowing down, getting ready for the U-turn that will turn him back to someone wearing a "Try God" T-shirt inside out.

Peter S. Hawkins

Notes

1. Tobias Wolff, ed., *Matters of Life and Death: New American Stories* (Green Harbor, Mass: Wampeter Press, 1983), xi.

2. Tobias Wolff, "Sister," *Back in the World* (Boston: Houghton Mifflin, 1985), 91.

3. Bonnie Lyons and Bill Oliver, "An Interview With Tobias Wolff," *Contemporary Literature* 31, no. 1 (Spring 1990): 15.

4. Lyons and Oliver, "An Interview with Tobias Wolff," 12.

5. "The Missing Person," *Back in the World,* 19.

6. "The Missing Person," 28.

7. "The Missing Person," 54.

8. Russell Banks, writing in the *New York Times Book Review* (October 20, 1985), cited by Marilyn C. Wesley, *Dictionary of Literary Biography*, vol. 130 (Detroit, Washington, D.C., London: Gale Research, 1993), 321.

9. Lyons and Oliver, 12.

The Rich Brother

There were two brothers, Pete and Donald.

Pete, the older brother, was in real estate. He and his wife had a Century 21 franchise in Santa Cruz. Pete worked hard and made a lot of money, but not any more than he thought he deserved. He had two daughters, a sailboat, a house from which he could see a thin slice of the ocean, and friends doing well enough in their own lives not to wish bad luck on him. Donald, the younger brother, was still single. He lived alone, painted houses when he found the work, and got deeper in debt to Pete when he didn't.

No one would have taken them for brothers. Where Pete was stout and hearty and at home in the world, Donald was bony, grave, and obsessed with the fate of his soul. Over the years Donald had worn the images of two different Perfect Masters around his neck. Out of devotion to the second of these he entered an ashram in Berkeley, where he nearly died of undiagnosed hepatitis. By the time Pete finished paying the medical bills Donald had become a Christian. He drifted from church to church, then joined a pentecostal community that met somewhere in the Mission District to sing in tongues and swap prophecies.

Pete couldn't make sense of it. Their parents were both dead, but while they were alive neither of them had found it necessary to believe in anything. They managed to be decent people without making fools of themselves, and Pete had the same ambition. He thought that the whole thing was an excuse for Donald to take himself seriously.

The trouble was that Donald couldn't content himself with worrying about his own soul. He had to worry about everyone else's, and especially Pete's. He handed down his judgments in ways that he seemed to consider subtle: through significant silence, innuendo, looks of mild despair that said, *Brother, what have you come to?* What Pete had come to, as far as he could tell, was prosperity. That was the real issue between them. Pete prospered and Donald did not prosper.

• • •

At the age of forty Pete took up sky diving. He made his first jump with two friends who'd started only a few months earlier and were already doing stunts. They were both coked to the gills when they jumped but Pete wanted to do it straight, at least the first time, and he was glad that he did. He would never have used the word *mystical*, but that was how Pete felt about the experience. Later he made the mistake of trying to describe it to Donald, who kept asking how much it cost and then acted appalled when Pete told him.

"At least I'm trying something new," Pete said. "At least I'm breaking the pattern."

Not long after that conversation Donald also broke the pattern, by going to live on a farm outside of Paso Robles. The farm was owned by several members of Donald's community, who had bought it and moved there with the idea of forming a family of faith. That was how Donald explained it in the first letter he sent. Every week Pete heard how happy Donald was, how "in the Lord." He told Pete that he was praying for him, he and the rest of Pete's brothers and sisters on the farm.

"I only have one brother," Pete wanted to answer, "and that's enough." But he kept this thought to himself.

In November the letters stopped. Pete didn't worry about this at first, but when he called Donald at Thanksgiving Donald was grim. He tried to sound upbeat but he didn't try hard enough to make it convincing. "Now listen," Pete said, "you don't have to stay in that place if you don't want to."

"I'll be all right," Donald answered.

"That's not the point. Being all right is not the point. If you don't like what's going on up there, then get out."

"I'm all right," Donald said again, more firmly. "I'm doing fine."

But he called Pete a week later and said that he was quitting the farm. When Pete asked him where he intended to go, Donald admitted that he had no plan. His car had been repossessed just before he left the city, and he was flat broke.

"I guess you'll have to stay with us," Pete said.

Donald put up a show of resistance. Then he gave in. "Just until I get my feet on the ground," he said.

"Right," Pete said. "Check out your options." He told Donald he'd send him money for a bus ticket, but as they were about to hang up Pete changed his mind. He knew that Donald would try hitchhiking to save the fare. Pete didn't want him out on the road all alone where some head case could pick him up, where anything could happen to him.

"Better yet," he said, "I'll come and get you."

"You don't have to do that. I didn't expect you to do that," Donald said. He added, "It's a pretty long drive."

"Just tell me how to get there."

But Donald wouldn't give him directions. He said that the farm was too depressing, that Pete wouldn't like it. Instead, he insisted on meeting Pete at a service station called Jonathan's Mechanical Emporium.

"You must be kidding," Pete said.

"It's close to the highway," Donald said. "I didn't name it."

"That's one for the collection," Pete said.

The day before he left to bring Donald home, Pete received a letter from a man who described himself as "head of household" at the farm where Donald had been living. From this letter Pete learned that Donald had not quit the farm, but had been asked to leave. The letter was written on the back of a mimeographed survey form asking people to record their response to a ceremony of some kind. The last question said:

What did you feel during the liturgy?
   a) Being
   b) Becoming
   c) Being and Becoming
   d) None of the Above
   e) All of the Above

Pete tried to forget the letter. But of course he couldn't. Each time he thought of it he felt crowded and breathless, a feeling that came over him again when he drove into the service station and saw Donald sitting against a wall with his head on his knees. It was late afternoon. A paper cup tumbled slowly past Donald's feet, pushed by the damp wind.

Pete honked and Donald raised his head. He smiled at Pete, then stood and stretched. His arms were long and thin and white. He wore a red bandanna across his forehead, a T-shirt with a couple of words on the front. Pete couldn't read them because the letters were inverted.

"Grow up," Pete yelled. "Get a Mercedes."

Donald came up to the window. He bent down and said, "Thanks for coming. You must be totally whipped."

"I'll make it." Pete pointed at Donald's T-shirt. "What's that supposed to say?"

Donald looked down at his shirt front. "Try God. I guess I put it on backwards. Pete, could I borrow a couple of dollars? I owe these people for coffee and sandwiches."

Pete took five twenties from his wallet and held them out the window.

Donald stepped back as if horrified. "I don't need that much."

"I can't keep track of all these nickels and dimes," Pete said. "Just pay me back when your ship comes in." He waved the bills impatiently. "Go on—take it."

"Only for now." Donald took the money and went into the service station office. He came out carrying two orange sodas, one of which he gave to Pete as he got into the car. "My treat," he said.

"No bags?"

"Wow, thanks for reminding me," Donald said. He balanced his drink on the dashboard, but the slight rocking of the car as he got out tipped it onto the passenger's seat, where half its contents foamed over before Pete could snatch it up again. Donald looked on while Pete held the bottle out the window, soda running down his fingers.

"Wipe it up," Pete told him. "Quick!"

"With what?"

Pete stared at Donald. "That shirt. Use the shirt."

Donald pulled a long face but did as he was told, his pale skin puckering against the wind.

"Great, just great," Pete said. "We haven't even left the gas station yet."

Afterwards, on the highway, Donald said, "This is a new car, isn't it?"

"Yes. This is a new car."

"Is that why you're so upset about the seat?"

"Forget it, okay? Let's just forget about it."

"I said I was sorry."

Pete said, "I just wish you'd be more careful. These seats are made of leather. That stain won't come out, not to mention the smell. I don't see why I can't have leather seats that smell like leather instead of orange pop."

"What was wrong with the other car?"

Pete glanced over at Donald. Donald had raised the hood of the blue sweatshirt he'd put on. The peaked hood above his gaunt, watchful face gave him the look of an inquisitor.

"There wasn't anything wrong with it," Pete said. "I just happened to like this one better."

Donald nodded.

There was a long silence between them as Pete drove on and the day darkened toward evening. On either side of the road lay stubble-covered fields. A line of low hills ran along the horizon, topped here and there with trees black against the grey sky. In the approaching line of cars a driver turned on his headlights. Pete did the same.

"So what happened?" he asked. "Farm life not your bag?"

Donald took some time to answer, and at last he said, simply, "It was my fault."

"What was your fault?"

"The whole thing. Don't play dumb, Pete. I know they wrote to you."
Donald looked at Pete, then stared out the windshield again.

"I'm not playing dumb."

Donald shrugged.

"All I really know is they asked you to leave," Pete went on. "I don't know any of the particulars."

"I blew it," Donald said. "Believe me, you don't want to hear the gory details."

"Sure I do," Pete said. He added, "Everybody likes the gory details."

"You mean everybody likes to hear how someone else messed up."

"Right," Pete said. "That's the way it is here on Spaceship Earth."

Donald bent one knee onto the front seat and leaned against the door so that he was facing Pete instead of the windshield. Pete was aware of Donald's scrutiny. He waited. Night was coming on in a rush now, filling the hollows of the land. Donald's long cheeks and deep-set eyes were dark with shadow. His brow was white. "Do you ever dream about me?" Donald asked.

"Do I ever dream about you? What kind of a question is that? Of course I don't dream about you," Pete said, untruthfully.

"What do you dream about?"

"Sex and money. Mostly money. A nightmare is when I dream I don't have any."

"You're just making that up," Donald said.

Pete smiled.

"Sometimes I wake up at night," Donald went on, "and I can tell you're dreaming about me."

"We were talking about the farm," Pete said. "Let's finish that conversation and then we can talk about our various out-of-body experiences and the interesting things we did during previous incarnations."

For a moment Donald looked like a grinning skull; then he turned serious again. "There's not that much to tell," he said. "I just didn't do anything right."

"That's a little vague," Pete said.

"Well, like the groceries. Whenever it was my turn to get the groceries I'd blow it somehow. I'd bring the groceries home and half of them would be missing, or I'd have all the wrong things, the wrong kind of flour or the wrong kind of chocolate or whatever. One time I gave them away. It's not funny, Pete."

Pete said, "Who did you give the groceries to?"

"Just some people I picked up on the way home. Some fieldworkers. They had about eight kids with them and they didn't even speak English—just nodded their heads. Still, I shouldn't have given away the groceries. Not all of them, anyway. I really learned my lesson about that. You have to be practical. You have to be fair to yourself." Donald leaned forward, and Pete could sense his excitement. "There's nothing actually wrong with being in business," he said. "As long as you're fair to other people you can still be fair to yourself. I'm thinking of going into business, Pete."

"We'll talk about it," Pete said. "So, that's the story? There isn't any more to it than that?"

"What did they tell you?" Donald asked.

"Nothing."

"They must have told you something."

Pete shook his head.

"They didn't tell you about the fire?" When Pete shook his head again Donald regarded him for a time, then said, "I don't know. It was stupid. I just completely lost it." He folded his arms across his chest and slumped back into the corner. "Everybody had to take turns cooking dinner. I usually did tuna casserole or spaghetti with garlic bread. But this one night I thought I'd do something different, something really interesting." Donald looked sharply at Pete. "It's all a big laugh to you, isn't it?"

"I'm sorry," Pete said.

"You don't know when to quit. You just keep hitting away."

"Tell me about the fire, Donald."

Donald kept watching him. "You have this compulsion to make me look foolish."

"Come off it, Donald. Don't make a big thing out of this."

"I know why you do it. It's because you don't have any purpose in life. You're afraid to relate to people who do, so you make fun of them."

"Relate," Pete said softly.

"You're basically a very frightened individual," Donald said. "Very threatened. You've always been like that. Do you remember when you used to try to kill me?"

"I don't have any compulsion to make you look foolish, Donald—you do it yourself. You're doing it right now."

"You can't tell me you don't remember," Donald said. "It was after my operation. You remember that."

"Sort of." Pete shrugged. "Not really."

"Oh yes," Donald said. "Do you want to see the scar?"

"I remember you had an operation. I don't remember the specifics, that's all. And I sure as hell don't remember trying to kill you."

"Oh yes," Donald repeated, maddeningly. "You bet your life you did. All the time. The thing was, I couldn't have anything happen to me where they sewed me up because then my intestines would come apart again and poison me. That was a big issue, Pete. Mom was always in a state about me climbing trees and so on. And you used to hit me there every chance you got."

"Mom was in a state every time you burped," Pete said. "I don't know. Maybe I bumped into you accidentally once or twice. I never did it deliberately."

"Every chance you got," Donald said. "Like when the folks went out at night and left you to baby-sit. I'd hear them say good night, and then I'd hear the car start up, and when they were gone I'd lie there and listen. After a while I would hear you coming down the hall, and I would close my eyes and pretend to be asleep. There were nights when you would stand outside the door, just stand there, and then go away again. But most nights you'd open the door and I would hear you in the room with me, breathing. You'd come over and sit next to me on the bed—you remember, Pete, you have to—you'd sit next to me on the bed and pull the sheets back. If I was on my stomach you'd roll me over. Then you would lift up my pajama shirt and start hitting me on my stitches. You'd hit me as hard as you could, over and over. And I would just keep lying there with my eyes closed. I was afraid that you'd get mad if you knew I was awake. Is that strange or what? I was afraid that you'd get mad if you found out that I knew you were trying to kill me." Donald laughed. "Come on, you can't tell me you don't remember that."

"It might have happened once or twice. Kids do those things. I can't get all excited about something I maybe did twenty-five years ago."

"No maybe about it. You did it."

Pete said, "You're wearing me out with this stuff. We've got a long drive ahead of us and if you don't back off pretty soon we aren't going to make it. You aren't, anyway."

Donald turned away.

"I'm doing my best," Pete said. The self-pity in his own voice made the words sound like a lie. But they weren't a lie! He was doing his best.

The car topped a rise. In the distance Pete saw a cluster of lights that blinked out when he started downhill. There was no moon. The sky was low and black.

"Come to think of it," Pete said, "I did have a dream about you the other night." Then he added, impatiently, as if Donald were badgering him, "A couple of other nights too. I'm getting hungry," he said.

"The same dream?"

"Different dreams. I only remember one of them well. There was something wrong with me, and you were helping out. Taking care of me. Just the two of us. I don't know where everyone else was supposed to be."

Pete left it at that. He didn't tell Donald that in this dream he was blind.

"I wonder if that was when I woke up," Donald said. He added, "I'm sorry I got into that thing about my scar. I keep trying to forget it but I guess I never will. Not really. It was pretty strange, having someone around all the time who wanted to get rid of me."

"Kid stuff," Pete said. "Ancient history."

They ate dinner at a Denny's on the other side of King City. As Pete was paying the check he heard a man behind him say, "Excuse me, but I wonder if I might ask which way you're going?" and Donald answer, "Santa Cruz."

"Perfect," the man said.

Pete could see him in the fish-eye mirror above the cash register: a red blazer with some kind of crest on the pocket, little black moustache, glossy black hair combed down on his forehead like a Roman emperor's. A rug, Pete thought. Definitely a rug.

Pete got his change and turned. "Why is that perfect?" he asked.

The man looked at Pete. He had a soft ruddy face that was doing its best to express pleasant surprise, as if this new wrinkle were all he could have wished for, but the eyes behind the aviator glasses showed signs of regret. His lips were moist and shiny. "I take it you're together," he said.

"You got it," Pete told him.

"All the better, then," the man went on. "It so happens I'm going to Santa Cruz myself. Had a spot of car trouble down the road. The old Caddy let me down."

"What kind of trouble?" Pete asked.

"Engine trouble," the man said. "I'm afraid it's a bit urgent. My daughter is sick. Urgently sick. I've got a telegram here." He patted the breast pocket of his blazer.

Pete grinned. Amazing, he thought, the old sick daughter ploy, but before he could say anything Donald got into the act again. "No problem," Donald said. "We've got tons of room."

"Not that much room," Pete said.

Donald nodded. "I'll put my things in the trunk."

"The trunk's full," Pete told him.

"It so happens I'm traveling light," the man said. "This leg of the trip anyway. In fact I don't have any luggage at this particular time."

Pete said, "Left it in the old Caddy, did you?"

"Exactly," the man said.

"No problem," Donald repeated. He walked outside and the man went with him. Together they strolled across the parking lot, Pete following at a distance. When they reached Pete's car Donald raised his face to the sky, and the man did the same. They stood there looking up. "Dark night," Donald said.

"Stygian," the man said.

Pete still had it in mind to brush him off, but he didn't do that. Instead he unlocked the door for him. He wanted to see what would happen. It was an adventure, but not a dangerous adventure. The man might steal Pete's ashtrays but he wouldn't kill him. If Pete got killed on the road it would be by some spiritual person in a sweatsuit, someone with his eyes on the far horizon and a wet Try God T-shirt in his duffel bag.

As soon as they left the parking lot the man lit a cigar. He blew a cloud of smoke over Pete's shoulder and sighed with pleasure. "Put it out," Pete told him.

"Of course," the man said. Pete looked into the rearview mirror and saw the man take another long puff before dropping the cigar out the window. "Forgive me," he said. "I should have asked. Name's Webster, by the way."

Donald turned and looked back at him. "First name or last?"

The man hesitated. "Last," he said finally.

"I know a Webster," Donald said. "Mick Webster."

"There are many of us," Webster said.

"Big fellow, wooden leg," Pete said.

Donald gave Pete a look.

Webster shook his head. "Doesn't ring a bell. Still, I wouldn't deny the connection. Might be one of the cousinry."

"What's your daughter got?" Pete asked.

"That isn't clear," Webster answered. "It appears to be a female complaint of some nature. Then again it may be tropical." He was quiet for a moment, and added: "If indeed it *is* tropical, I will have to assume some of the blame myself. It was my own vaulting ambition that first led us to the tropics and kept us in the tropics all those many years, exposed to every evil. Truly I have much to answer for. I left my wife there."

Donald said quietly, "You mean she died?"

"I buried her with these hands. The earth will be repaid, gold for gold."

"Which tropics?" Pete asked.

"The tropics of Peru."

"What part of Peru are they in?"

"The lowlands," Webster said.

Pete nodded. "What's it like down there?"

"Another world," Webster said. His tone was sepulchral. "A world better imagined than described."

"Far out," Pete said.

The three men rode in silence for a time. A line of trucks went past in the other direction, trailers festooned with running lights, engines roaring.

"Yes," Webster said at last, "I have much to answer for."

Pete smiled at Donald, but Donald had turned in his seat again and was gazing at Webster. "I'm sorry about your wife," Donald said.

"What did she die of?" Pete asked.

"A wasting illness," Webster said. "The doctors have no name for it, but I do." He leaned forward and said, fiercely, "*Greed.*" Then he slumped back against his seat. "My greed, not hers. She wanted no part of it."

Pete bit his lip. Webster was a find and Pete didn't want to scare him off by hooting at him. In a voice low and innocent of knowingness, he asked, "What took you there?"

"It's difficult for me to talk about."

"Try," Pete told him.

"A cigar would make it easier."

Donald turned to Pete and said, "It's okay with me."

"All right," Pete said. "Go ahead. Just keep the window rolled down."

"Much obliged." A match flared. There were eager sucking sounds.

"Let's hear it," Pete said.

"I am by training an engineer," Webster began. "My work has exposed me to all but one of the continents, to desert and alp and forest, to every terrain and season of the earth. Some years ago I was hired by the Peruvian government to search for tungsten in the tropics. My wife and daughter accompanied me. We were the only white people for a thousand miles in any direction, and we had no choice but to live as the Indians lived—to share their food and drink and even their culture."

Pete said, "You knew the lingo, did you?"

"We picked it up." The ember of the cigar bobbed up and down. "We were used to learning as necessity decreed. At any rate, it became evident after a couple of years that there was no tungsten to be found. My wife had fallen ill and was pleading to be taken home. But I was deaf to her pleas, because by then I was on the trail of another metal—a metal far more valuable than tungsten."

"Let me guess," Pete said. "Gold?"

Donald looked at Pete, then back at Webster.

"Gold," Webster said. "A vein of gold greater than the Mother Lode itself. After I found the first traces of it nothing could tear me away from my search—not the sickness of my wife nor anything else. I was determined to uncover the vein, and so I did—but not before I laid my wife to rest. As I say, the earth will be repaid."

Webster was quiet. Then he said, "But life must go on. In the years since my wife's death I have been making the arrangements necessary to open the mine. I could have done it immediately, of course, enriching myself beyond measure, but I knew what that would mean—the exploitation of our beloved Indians, the brutal destruction of their environment. I felt I had too much to atone for already." Webster paused, and when he spoke again his voice was dull and rushed, as if he had used up all the interest he had in his own words. "Instead I drew up a program for returning the bulk of the wealth to the Indians themselves. A kind of trust fund. The interest alone will allow them to secure their ancient lands and rights in perpetuity. At the same time, our investors will be rewarded a thousandfold. Two-thousandfold. Everyone will prosper together."

"That's great," Donald said. "That's the way it ought to be."

Pete said, "I'm willing to bet that you just happen to have a few shares left. Am I right?"

Webster made no reply.

"Well?" Pete knew that Webster was on to him now, but he didn't care. The story had bored him. He'd expected something different, something original, and Webster had let him down. He hadn't even tried. Pete felt sour and stale. His eyes burned from cigar smoke and the high beams of road-hogging truckers. "Douse the stogie," he said to Webster. "I told you to keep the window down."

"Got a little nippy back here."

Donald said, "Hey, Pete. Lighten up."

"Douse it!"

Webster sighed. He got rid of the cigar.

"I'm a wreck," Pete said to Donald. "You want to drive for a while?"

Donald nodded.

Pete pulled over and they changed places.

Webster kept his counsel in the back seat. Donald hummed while he drove, until Pete told him to stop. Then everything was quiet.

Donald was humming again when Pete woke up. Pete stared sullenly at the road, at the white lines sliding past the car. After a few moments of this he turned and said, "How long have I been out?"

Donald glanced at him. "Twenty, twenty-five minutes."

Pete looked behind him and saw that Webster was gone. "Where's our friend?"

"You just missed him. He got out in Soledad. He told me to say thanks and good-bye."

"Soledad? What about his sick daughter? How did he explain her away?" Pete leaned over the seat. Both ashtrays were still in place. Floor mats. Door handles.

"He has a brother living there. He's going to borrow a car from him and drive the rest of the way in the morning."

I'll bet his brother's living there," Pete said. "Doing fifty concurrent life sentences. His brother and his sister and his mom and his dad."

"I kind of liked him," Donald said.

"I'm sure you did," Pete said wearily.

"He was interesting. He'd been places."

"His cigars had been places, I'll give you that."

"Come on, Pete."

"Come on yourself. What a phony."

"You don't know that."

"Sure I do."

"How? How do you know?"

Pete stretched. "Brother, there are some things you're just born knowing. What's the gas situation?"

"We're a little low."

"Then why didn't you get some more?"

"I wish you wouldn't snap at me like that," Donald said.

"Then why don't you use your head? What if we run out?"

"We'll make it," Donald said. "I'm pretty sure we've got enough to make it. You didn't have to be so rude to him," Donald added.

Pete took a deep breath. "I don't feel like running out of gas tonight, okay?"

Donald pulled in at the next station they came to and filled the tank while Pete went to the men's room. When Pete came back, Donald was sitting in the passenger's seat. The attendant came up to the driver's window as Pete got in behind the wheel. He bent down and said, "Twelve fifty-five."

"You heard the man," Pete said to Donald.

Donald looked straight ahead. He didn't move.

"Cough up," Pete said. "This trip's on you."

Donald said, softly, "I can't."

"Sure you can. Break out that wad."

Donald glanced up at the attendant, then at Pete. "Please," he said. "Pete, I don't have it anymore."

Pete took this in. He nodded, and paid the attendant.

Donald began to speak when they left the station but Pete cut him off. He said, "I don't want to hear from you right now. You just keep quiet or I swear to God I won't be responsible."

They left the fields and entered a tunnel of tall trees. The trees went on and on. "Let me get this straight," Pete said at last. "You don't have the money I gave you."

"You treated him like a bug or something," Donald said.

"You don't have the money," Pete said again.

Donald shook his head.

"Since I bought dinner, and since we didn't stop anywhere in between, I assume you gave it to Webster. Is that right? Is that what you did with it?"

"Yes."

Pete looked at Donald. His face was dark under the hood but he still managed to convey a sense of remove, as if none of this had anything to do with him.

"Why?" Pete asked. "Why did you give it to him?" When Donald didn't answer, Pete said, "A hundred dollars. Gone. Just like that. I *worked* for that money, Donald."

"I know, I know," Donald said.

"You don't know! How could you? You get money by holding out your hand."

"I work too," Donald said.

"You work too. Don't kid yourself, brother."

Donald leaned toward Pete, about to say something but Pete cut him off again.

"You're not the only one on the payroll, Donald. I don't think you understand that. I have a family."

"Pete, I'll pay you back."

"Like hell you will. A hundred dollars!" Pete hit the steering wheel with the palm of his hand. "Just because you think I hurt some goofball's feelings. Jesus, Donald."

"That's not the reason," Donald said. "And I didn't just *give* him the money."

"What do you call it, then? What do you call what you did?"

"I *invested* it. I wanted a share, Pete." When Pete looked over at him Donald nodded and said again, "I wanted a share."

Pete said, "I take it you're referring to the gold mine in Peru."

"Yes," Donald said.

"You believe that such a gold mine exists?"

Donald looked at Pete, and Pete could see him just beginning to catch on. "You'll believe anything," Pete said. "Won't you? You really will believe anything at all."

"I'm sorry," Donald said, and turned away.

Pete drove on between the trees and considered the truth of what he had just said—that Donald would believe anything at all. And it came to him that it would be just like this unfair life for Donald to come out ahead in the end, by believing in some outrageous promise that would turn out to be true and that he, Pete, would reject out of hand because he was too wised up to listen to anybody's pitch anymore except for laughs. What a joke. What a joke if there really was a blessing to be had, and the blessing didn't come to the one who deserved it, the one who did all the work, but to the other.

And as if this had already happened Pete felt a shadow move upon him, darkening his thoughts. After a time he said, "I can see where all this is going, Donald."

"I'll pay you back," Donald said.

"No," Pete said. "You won't pay me back. You can't. You don't know how. All you've ever done is take. All your life."

Donald shook his head.

"I see exactly where this is going," Pete went on. "You can't work, you can't take care of yourself, you believe anything anyone tells you. I'm stuck with you, aren't I?" He looked over at Donald. "I've got you on my hands for good."

Donald pressed his fingers against the dashboard as if to brace himself. "I'll get out," he said.

Pete kept driving.

"Let me out," Donald said. "I mean it, Pete."

"Do you?"

Donald hesitated. "Yes," he said.

"Be sure," Pete told him. "This is it. This is for keeps."

"I mean it."

"All right. You made the choice." Pete braked the car sharply and swung it to the shoulder of the road. He turned off the engine and got out. Trees loomed on both sides, shutting out the sky. The air was cold and musty. Pete took Donald's duffel bag from the back seat and set it down behind the car. He stood there, facing Donald in the red glow of the taillights. "It's better this way," Pete said.

Donald just looked at him.

"Better for you," Pete said.

Donald hugged himself. He was shaking. "You don't have to say all that," he told Pete. "I don't blame you."

"Blame me? What the hell are you talking about? Blame me for what?"

"For anything," Donald said.

"I want to know what you mean by blame me."

"Nothing. Nothing, Pete. You'd better get going. God bless you."

"That's it," Pete said. He dropped to one knee, searching the packed dirt with his hands. He didn't know what he was looking for; his hands would know when they found it.

Donald touched Pete's shoulder. "You'd better go," he said.

Somewhere in the trees Pete heard a branch snap. He stood up. He looked at Donald, then went back to the car and drove away. He drove fast, hunched over the wheel, conscious of the way he was hunched and the shallowness of his breathing, refusing to look at the mirror above his head until there was nothing behind him but darkness.

Then he said, "A hundred dollars," as if there were someone to hear.

The trees gave way to fields. Metal fences ran beside the road, plastered with windblown scraps of paper. Tule fog hung above the ditches, spilling into the road, dimming the ghostly halogen lights that burned in the yards of the farms Pete passed. The fog left beads of water rolling up the windshield.

Pete rummaged among his cassettes. He found Pachelbel's Canon and pushed it into the tape deck. When the violins began to play he leaned back and assumed an attentive expression as if he were really listening to them. He smiled to himself like a man at liberty to enjoy music, a man who has finished his work and settled his debts, done all things meet and due.

And in this way, smiling, nodding to the music, he went another mile or so and pretended that he was not already slowing down, that he was not going to turn back, that he would be able to drive on like this, alone, and have the right answer when his wife stood before him in the doorway of his home and asked, Where is he? Where is your brother?

From *Back in the World* by Tobias Wolff. Copyright © 1981 by Tobias Wolff. Reprinted by permission of International Creative Management, Inc.

Guides to Reflection

1. Discuss the clash of character types Wolff is constructing in his contrast between these two brothers.

2. Pete denies that he ever dreams about Donald, but only about "Sex and money. Mostly money" *(Reader, 75)*. And yet we later learn that Pete, in fact, did dream about being blind and being taken care of by Donald. What might be the significance of this? Is it in any way related to the "ancient history" the two brothers share, the flip side of Pete's trying to hurt, perhaps even kill, Donald when the two were boys?

3. Webster is one of Wolff's more obvious liars. How does he function in this story?

4. A biblically literate reader will recognize the way in which Wolff tells his story against the background of Scripture: Cain and Abel, Esau and Jacob, the two brothers of the parable in Luke 15, as well as Mary and Martha. How does the Bible enrich your reading of this story? Is it necessary to have these biblical subtexts in mind to enjoy or understand "The Rich Brother"?

5. In speaking about this story with interviewers, Tobias Wolff was willing to consider Pete's decision to return to Donald as "an intervention of grace"; but he also insisted that instead of being some kind of violent eruption out of heaven, it was "a natural psychological event" in Pete's life.[1] Discuss these distinctions between the spiritual and the psychological. How do they correspond to your own experience of grace?

6. Discuss Pete's conjecture: "What a joke if there really was a blessing to be had, and the blessing didn't come to the one who deserved it, the one who did all the work, but to the other" *(Reader, 83-84)*.

Notes

1. Bonnie Lyons and Bill Oliver, "An Interview With Tobias Wolff," *Contemporary Literature* 31, no. 1 (Spring 1990): 12-13.

5

Carol Bly

Carol Bly is a writer with a moral passion: she wants to reorient modern literature, to convince contemporary writers of short stories and novels that their work is crippled by a lack of ethical vision. Bly's urgent, challenging voice first found a vehicle in the essay form. Her "Letters from the Country" appeared in *Minnesota Monthly* throughout the 1970s and were collected in a book by the same name and published by Harper and Row in 1981. In these essays, Bly reported on rural life from her home in western Minnesota, often celebrating the natural beauty of Lac Qui Parle County, while also lamenting or lambasting the narrow blindness of its political, social, and religious life.

For the past 15 years, Bly's primary form of expression has been the short story rather than the essay, which she says is "3000% easier to write than a short story."[1] She has, however, augmented her two collections of stories, *Backbone* (1985) and *The Tomcat's Wife* (1991), with an extended essay entitled "Bad Government and Silly Literature" (1986) and a book on how to write stories titled *The Passionate, Accurate Story: Making Your Heart's Truth into Literature* (1990). Bly has also co-authored *Soil and Survival: Land Stewardship and the Future of American Agriculture* (1986) and edited *Everybody's Story: Writing by Older Minnesotans* (1987). Many of Bly's stories from this period are set in northern Minnesota, and some have been adapted for an American Playhouse film, *Rachel River*.

Bly's desire to reform contemporary writing comes from her conviction that "the world desperately needs public-minded literature"[2] in the tradition of Leo Tolstoy and Albert Camus. She believes that such a literature would bring an "*ethical* wakening"[3] to American culture, whose government she sees as too often fostering "appalling foreign and domestic policy."[4] Decrying the predominantly aesthetic interest of most writers now, Bly condemns "silvery little stories made up of shards of experience, quickly picked up, experienced by the reader the way a jogger sees the glitter of mica in clay."[5] She says writers of such stories focus on small details—"grass from the mower blade, oil spitting in a pan, congealed eggs on one's plate"[6]—and give scant notice to moral issues in the characters' lives. At best, the stories evoke the thin affairs of privileged people, describing how "Radcliffe characters are getting along with ... Harvard characters."[7] Technically aglitter, the stories ride on plots "full of people who role-model avarice and violence and have no sense of world community."[8]

Bly claims that editorial preferences ("Put it in the present tense to make *The New Yorker*"[9]) hold writers back from exploring ethical questions in their work. So too, she claims, does what some ethicists call the "Bystander Effect": "Our friends aren't writing novels about how nice Andover and Yale graduates love literature but govern unkindly, so we don't write the book either."[10] Instead, writers dwell on developing technical skill in describing small physical effects and sketching shallow relationships.

To combat the "moral drift"[11] that produces such stories, Bly recommends that all writers compose what she calls a "Values Listing" before they write. These lists will, she hopes, keep the writers' sights on the ethical issues that concern virtually everybody but that seem difficult for many to write about. Categories on Bly's listing include goals or values that make life good or bearable, goals or values that cause injustice or suffering, goals or behaviors that are missing, and injustices that you see about you and should keep an eye on, even on your wedding day.[12] What she calls "the most heartfelt" of her own Values List is "the fact that not individual people but large corporations, groups, and government agencies do the terrifying evil of our time. In fact, organizations—not we individual people—endanger the earth itself. Yet, top level members of these organizations and the spouses who sleep with them, apparently feel no remorse. They are short-term profiting off the earth."[13] Bly believes that an entry like this one on a Values Listing will allow an author to write literature that helps readers encounter significant ethical issues. This literature may also motivate them to act upon the convictions arising from those encounters.

With a strong, pointed voice, Bly urges writers to resist the English teachers, family, neighbors, and clergy who shy away from confronting large evils. In her view, writers who want to be true to their calling and craft must overcome such comfortable timidity. Sometimes strident in her cause, always challenging, Bly is passionately committed to a reform of literature that she sees as crucial to the well-being of people in the world.

Turning from Bly's essays to her stories, one may see shadows of her Values Listing. In the stories in *The Tomcat's Wife*, for instance, we see the physical and emotional abuse of wives and children by husbands and fathers, a landlord's theft of welfare checks from old tenants, various infidelities, and the smooth insensitivity of a rich prep school administrator to a group of poor foster children. All are problems that recall Bly's moral dismay at injustice and suffering. The religious people—lay and clergy—who appear frequently in these stories sometimes perpetrate these evils, sometimes rescue victims from assailants, and sometimes stand by as others suffer. In "After the Baptism," the suffering of characters is not as immediately acute as in some of the other stories in *The Tomcat's Wife*. Nonetheless, even though blunted by ceremony, social class, and physical distance, the evils that so disturb Bly do in fact fuel this story of an infant girl's baptism.

Set in a "tacky suburb," the story revolves around a grandfather's effort to make his grandchild's baptism "beautiful" and "successful" *(Reader, 95, 91, 94)*—that is, an aesthetically pleasing and socially satisfying event. The owner of a chemical company that produces nerve gas, the grandfather is an adept administrator who efficiently negotiates the problems of baptism "when most of the religion is gone while the custom lives on," when "no one with an IQ over one hundred" *(Reader, 95, 91)* actually believes what the priest says about the sacrament. Complicating the situation further for the grandfather are the insipidity of the priest and some guests, the difference in social class between his son and the son's wife, the appearance outside the reception of protesters against the production of nerve gas, the cruelty of various family members to each other, and the crime his son committed several years earlier. The social, political, and religious worlds Bly presents in the story are all deeply flawed. The evils influencing the characters' lives are potent and seemingly entrenched.

Despite the grandfather's attention to detail, one unplanned event occurs at the reception after the baptism: a godmother to the baby tells a story about her marriage. In this story, and its echoes in other characters' lives, lie possible hopes for addressing the evils that otherwise seem so strong. But the hopes may lack the evils' strength, and they are held in check by the godmother's response to the promise of baptism: "And how is flesh ever safe?" *(Reader, 103)*. For some characters in Bly's story, this question echoes in a hollow shell of an outmoded religion that is unwilling to face real questions about evil, suffering, and death. For others, however, the luminous if ephemeral moments of hope, like wind-driven dust and cleansing rain that marks the end of the baptismal reception, may suggest something more—a distant but possible response to questions about fragile flesh and potent evil.

Paula J. Carlson

Notes

1. Carol Bly, *The Passionate, Accurate Story: Making Your Heart's Truth into Literature* (Minneapolis: Milkweed Editions, 1990), 23.

2. *The Passionate, Accurate Story,* 9.

3. Carol Bly, "Bad Government and Silly Literature: An Essay" (Minneapolis: Milkweed Editions, 1986), 22.

4. "Bad Government and Silly Literature," 19.

5. *The Passionate, Accurate Story,* 6.

6. *The Passionate, Accurate Story,* 6.

7. "Bad Government and Silly Literature," 18.

8. *The Passionate, Accurate Story,* 39.

9. *The Passionate, Accurate Story,* 6.

10. "Bad Government and Silly Literature," 19.

11. "Bad Government and Silly Literature," 22.

12. *The Passionate, Accurate Story,* 39-40.

13. *The Passionate, Accurate Story,* 40.

After the Baptism

The Benty Family had a beautiful baptism for their baby—when a good deal might have gone wrong. It is hard to run any baptism these days: of all the fifty-odd Episcopalians in Saint Aidan's Church, not to mention the two Lutheran grandparents, who really believes much of what the young priest says? No one with an IQ over one hundred actually supposes that "baptism could never be more truly, truly relevant than it is right now, in our day and age." People may get a kick out of the rhetoric, but that doesn't mean they believe it. If Bill Benty, Senior, the baby's grandfather, tried any of that proclaiming style of Father Geoffrey, if he tried anything like that just once over at the plant, he'd be laughed out to the fence in two minutes.

At least Father Geoffrey was long enough out of seminary now so he'd left off pronouncing Holy Ghost Ha-oly Gha-ost. His delivery was clear and manly. When he took the baby from her godparents, he took hold of her in a no-nonsense way: her mussed, beautiful white skirts billowed over his arm like sail being carried to the water. But the man was vapid. A frank, charming midwestern accent can't bring dead ideas to life. He had been charming about agreeing on the 1928 baptism service, instead of the 1979. Bill's wife, Lois, loved the beautiful old phrasing. Beautiful it was, too, Bill thought now, but on the other hand, how could any realistic person ask those particular three godparents "to renounce the vain pomp and glory of the world"? Where would that crew get any glory from in the first place?

The middle-aged godparent was Bill's long-lost first cousin, Molly Wells. Thirty-odd years ago she had run away to North Carolina to marry. After almost no correspondence in all those years, Molly had shown up widowed—a thin, sad woman with white hair done in what Lois called your bottom-line, bodywave-only permanent. Neither Bill nor Lois had met her husband. Bill had mailed her Dittoed, and later photocopied, Christmas letters, as he did to all his relations, giving news of Lois's work in Episcopal Community Services and whatever of interest there was to say about the chemical plant, and young Will's graduations and accomplishments—Breck School, Reed, the Harvard B School, his first marriage, his job with the arts organization before the snafu, his marriage to Cheryl. Molly and her husband had no children, and her responses to the Bentys' news were scarcely more than southern-lady thank-you notes.

Then in July of this long, very hot summer, she announced she was now widowed and would visit. Here she was, a houseguest who kept to her room, considerate enough not to dampen their family joking with her grief. Today, for the baptism, she wore a two-piece pink dress, gloves, and a straw-brimmed hat. Since one expects a young face under a broad-brimmed hat, Bill had had a moment's quake to see Molly, when she came down the staircase that morning. Molly had frankly told them she had not darkened the doorway of a church in thirty years but she would not disgrace them.

The other godparents were an oldish young couple whom Will dug up from his remaining high-school acquaintance. Bill had warned Will that you had to give these things time: when a man has been caught embezzling he must allow his friends months, even a year, to keep saying how sorry they are, but the fact is, they can't really ever look at him the same way again. For a good two or three years they will still mention to people that he was caught embezzling or whatever, but in fact they have no rancor left themselves. In about five years, they will again be affectionate friends but never as in the first place. It was only a question of having the sense not to ask them for help getting a job the first two years—and then simply to wait.

Probably Will was lucky to have found this couple, Chad and Jodi Plathe, to stand up for his baby. They were not Episcopalians. They were meditators, and if not actually organic farmers, at least organic eaters. When Will and Cheryl brought them over to Bill and Lois's for dinner earlier in the month, it had been fun to goad them. Each time Chad mentioned an interest of theirs, Bill had said, "Oh, then it follows you must be into organic eating." Or "Oh, then it follows you must be into horoscopes." "Into Sufi dancing, I bet." They were—into all the philosophies he brought up. They looked at him, puzzled, and young Will said, "Very witty, Dad—oh, witty." Once Chad said something hostile back, Bill forgave him everything. In one sense, Bill had rather listen to a non-Christian fallen-away Bay Area Buddhist who is man enough to take offense, at least, than to this Father Geoffrey, with his everlasting love for everything and everybody.

Now Chad and Jodi stood at the font, their backs to the grandparents in the first row and all the congregation in the next rows. They wore their eternal blue jeans, with the tops of plastic sandwich bags sticking out of the back pockets. They wore 1960s-style rebozos with earth-tone embroidery and rust-colored sewn-on doves. Their shoulder-length hair was shiny and combed. At least, Bill thought comfortably, very little evil in the world was generated by vegetarians. He saved up that idea to tell Chad if the conversation dragged at dinner.

Early that morning, Bill had taken his coffee happily out into the little back-kitchen screened porch. The wind was down, and the ivy's thousands of hide claws held the screens peacefully. Like all true householders, Bill liked being up while others slept. His wide lawn lay shadowed under four elms the city hadn't had to take down yet. The grass showed a pale gleam of dew and looked more beautiful than it really was. Across the avenue, where the large grounds of Benty Chem started, Bill had ordered a landscaping outfit to put in generous groupings of fine high bushes and hundreds of perennials. He ordered them planted on both sides of the fence. Now that it was August, and everything had taken hold, the grounds looked lavender and gentle.

"You can't make a chemical factory look like an Englishman's estate," Lois had told him last week. "But, darling, darn near! Darn near! If only the protesters would wear battered stovepipe hats and black scarves!"

Bill told her that he had heard at a Saint Aidan's Vestry meeting that the protesting or peace-demonstrating community of the Twin Cities definitely regarded Benty Chem as a lot more beautiful place to work around than any one of Honeywell's layouts. "And they should know," Bill added with satisfaction.

At seven-thirty, the usual Sunday contingent of protesters weren't on the job yet. It was generally Sue Ann and Mary, or Sue Ann and Drew, on Sundays. Bill learned their first names automatically, as he learned the first names of new janitorial staff at Benty Chem. Now he gathered himself, got into the car, and was out at Northwest Cargo Recovery on Thirty-fourth Street in good time. He signed for the lobsters. They were moving around a little, safe, greenish-black, in their plastic carrying case. "Hi, fellows and girls!" he said good-naturedly to them. He felt the luggage people smiling at him from behind their counter. Bill knew he was more spontaneous and humorous than most people they dealt with. "For my first grandchild's baptism!" he told them.

When he got home, the caterers had come. Lois was fingering along the bookcases, looking for the extra 1928 prayer books. Molly sat, cool in her silk two-piece dress. "I do believe it's threatening rain," she said in her partly southern accent. "Oh, and rain is just so much needed by our farmers." Her "our farmers" sounded false, feudal even, but Bill said, "Darn right, Molly!"

Now he relaxed in church. He flung an arm around the bench end, a little figure carved in shallow relief. Some Episcopalian in Bill's dad's generation had brought six of these carvings from Norfolk. They all cracked during their first winter of American central heating. Bill and a couple of other vestrymen glued the cracks and set vises; then they mortised in hardwood tholes against the grain, to make them safe forever. Each bench end was a small monk, with robe, hood, and cinch. The medieval sculptor had made the little monks hold their glossy wooden hands up, nearly touching their noses, in prayer. The faces had no particular expression.

Bill sat more informally than other people in Saint Aidan's. He had the peaceful slouch of those who are on the inside, the ones who know the workings behind some occasion, like cooks for a feast, or vestrymen for a service, or grandfathers for a baptism. Bill had done a lot of work and thinking to make this baptism successful, so now his face was pleasant and relaxed. He was aware of the Oppedahls next to him, the baby's other grandparents, sweating out the Episcopal service that they disliked. He thought they were darn good sports. He leaned across Lois at one point and whispered to Merv Oppedahl that a strong Scotch awaited the stalwart fellow that got through all the Smells and Bells. Merv's face broke into a grin, and he made a thumbs-up with the hand that wasn't holding Doreen's hand.

All summer the wretched farmers' topsoil had been lifting and lifting, then moving into the suburbs, even into Saint Paul itself. Grit stuck to people's foreheads and screens, even to the woven metal of their fences. But inside Saint Aidan's, the air was high and cool; the clerestory windows, thank heavens, were not the usual dark- and royal-blue and dark-rose stained-glass imitations of Continental cathedral windows—full of symbols of lions for Saint Mark and eagles for Saint John, which a whole generation of Episcopalians didn't know anything about, anyway. Besides, they made churches dark. Saint Aidan's had a good deal of clear glass, and enough gold-stained windows so that all the vaulting looked rather gold and light. It was an oddly watery look. In fact, the church reminded Bill of the insides of the overturned canoe of his childhood. It had been made of varnished ribs and strakes; when the boys turned it over and dove down to come up inside it, madly treading water, they felt transformed by that watery arching. It was a spooky yellow-dark. No matter that at ten their voices must still have been unchanged; they shouted all the rhetoric and bits of poems they knew. They made everything pontifical. They made dire prophecies. They felt portentous about death, even. Not the sissy, capon death they taught you about at Cass Lake Episcopal Camp, but the death that would get you if a giant pried your fists off the thwarts and shoved you down.

Now Father Geoffrey was done with the godparents. He put his thumb into the palm oil and pressed it onto the baby's forehead. Then he cried in a full voice, "I pronounce you, Molly Oppedahl Benty, safe in our Lord Jesus Christ forever!" Tears made some people's eyes brittle. They all sang "Love divine, all loves excel-l-l-ling ..." using the Hyfrodol tune. Then it was noon, and they could leave.

Everyone tottered across the white, spiky gravel of the parking lot. They called out unnecessary friendly words from car to car. "See you at the Bentys' in five minutes, then!" and "Beautiful service, wasn't it?" "Anyone need a ride? We can certainly take two more!"

The cars full of guests drove companionably across the tacky suburb. People felt happy in different ways, but all of them felt more blessed than the people they passed. They may have been to a sacrament that they didn't much believe in, but they at least had been to one. Ten years before, all these streets had been shadowy under the elms. Now, though spindly maple saplings stood guyed in their steel-mesh cages, the town showed itself dispirited in its lidless houses that human beings build and live in. The open garages, with here and there a man pottering about, looked more inviting than the houses. The men tinkered in the hot shadow, handling gigantic mowing and spraying equipment parked there. No one could imagine a passion happening in the houses—not even a mild mid-life crisis. Not even a hobby, past an assembled kit.

Another reason everyone felt contented was that all their troubles with one another had been worked out the week before. Unbeatable, humane, wise, experienced administrator that he was, Bill explained to Lois, he had done the best possible thing to guarantee them all a great baptism Sunday by having Will and Cheryl (and little Molly) over to dinner the week before. There were always tensions about religious occasions. The tensions are all the worse when most of the religion is gone while the custom lives on. Each detail of the custom—what's in good taste and what's the way we've always done it before—is a bloodletting issue. Now, there were two things to do about bloodletting issues, Bill told Lois.

"Yes, dear?" she said with a smile.

"If the issues can be solved to anyone's satisfaction, just solve them. But if they can't be solved at all, have the big fight about them a week ahead. Then everybody is sick of fighting by the time you have the occasion itself."

Lois said, "Makes sense. What can't be solved, though?"

He gave her a look. "Our son and our daughter-in-law are not very happily married. They started a baby two months before they married. And you and I will always just have to hope that it was Will's idea to marry Cheryl and not Merv Oppedahl's idea at the end of a magnum. Next: Cheryl wanted the baby to be named Chereen—a combo of Cheryl, for herself, and Doreen, for her mother. Our son thinks Chereen is a disgusting idea. Next: Cheryl puts a descant onto any hymn we sing, including—if I remember correctly, and I am afraid I will never forget—onto 'Jesu, Joy of Man's Desiring' and Beethoven's Ninth, whatever that one is."

"'Hymn to Joy,'" Lois said.

"'Hymn to Joy,'" Bill said. "Next: The Oppedahls are probably not very happy that their daughter has married someone who did two years at Sandstone Federal Prison for embezzlement. Next: You and I are not happy about Will's marrying Cheryl. She is tasteless. He is mean to her. Are you with me so far? Then next is the choice of godparents. Good grief! It is nice that Will wants to honor his second cousin Molly Wells by asking her to stand godparent, but she hasn't gone to church in thirty years. And Cheryl wanted a young couple, not an old great-aunt, for her baby's sponsors. It is obvious Will chose Molly because she gave them seventeen thousand dollars by way of a nest egg. Very handsome thing to do. *Very* handsome, considering Will's record."

Lois said, "Oh, dear, must you?"

"All these things are on people's minds. It's best to have it all out ahead of time. Just because a rich aunt gives someone money is not a reason for having her stand godmother—especially when the baby's mother obviously doesn't want it. Next: The Oppedahls aren't going to be comfortable with the Episcopal Church service, but they'd be a sight *more* comfortable if we used the modern language of 1979—but the baby's grandmother on the other side wants 1928."

Lois said, "Oh, dear. I thought *I* was going to come out of this clean."

Bill laughed, "No one comes out of a family fight clean. Next: Mrs. Oppedahl is a horrible cold fish who doesn't like anybody. She doesn't even like her own daughter very well. In fact—poor Cheryl! Do you know what she told me? She told me the first time she ever felt popular, as she put it, was at Lutheran Bible camp, when all the girls discovered she could harmonize to the hymns. Suddenly it made her part of the group. When they all got back from camp, the girls talked about her as if she were someone that counted, and the boys picked up on it. She was O.K. in high school after that. She told me that just that one Lutheran Bible Camp gave her more nourishment—her word—than she'd ever got from her parents."

"You're a wonder, dear," Lois said. "What about the other godparents?"

"The holistic birdseed-eaters? They know perfectly well that the only reason Will chose them was to override any chance of Cheryl's having some couple *she'd* choose. They know that I think their knee-jerk Gaya stuff is silly, and they will feel awkward about the service. I don't know what to do about them."

Lois said, "We will have lobsters. That's not meat! Then they won't bring their plastic bags of whatever."

"Boiled live lobster. Great idea. They will eat it or I will shove it down their throats," Bill said. "I will offend Doreen Oppedahl by offering Merv a strong drink. It'll buck him up, and she's hopeless, anyway."

"Have we thought of everything?" Lois said.

Bill turned serious a moment. "I am going to tell Will he can't speak cruelly to his wife in my house."

Lois said, "Well, poor Will! Do you remember how when we were all somewhere, at someone's house, suddenly there was Cheryl telling everyone how she and Will met because they were both at the microfiche in the public library together and they both felt sick from the fiche?"

"Nothing wrong with that," Bill said. "Microfiche does make people feel like throwing up."

"But she went on and on about how nausea had brought them together!"

Bill said, "I remember. Will told her to shut up, too, right in front of everyone."

The week before the baptism, therefore, Will and Cheryl and little Molly joined Bill, Lois, and their cousin Molly Wells for dinner. They aired grievances, just as Bill had planned. Then he glanced out the window and said to his son, "Come on out and help me with the protesters, Will."

Everyone looked out. The usual Sunday protesters had been on the opposite sidewalk, near the plant fence. They looked flagged from the heat, but determined. Bill saw it was Sue Ann and Polly this time. They had their signs turned so they could be read from the Benty house. IT IS HARD TO BE PROUD OF CHEMICAL WARFARE was the message for that Sunday. Now the two young people had moved to this side of the avenue, doing the westward reach of their loop on the public sidewalk but taking the eastward reach on Bill and Lois's lawn.

"Not on my lawn they don't," Bill said, smiling equably at the others. "We'll be right back."

Father and son went to the lawn edge and stood side by side, waiting for the protesters to come up abreast of where they were. The women, in the house, could see their backs but couldn't hear what was said. Presently they realized nothing violent seemed likely. They made out the protesters smiling, and Bill turned slightly, apparently calling a parting shot of some civil kind to them. The protesters moved back over to the Benty Chemical side of the street, and Will and Bill came across the lawn toward the house.

Bill had used that time to speak to his son. "I can't stop you from treating your wife rudely in your own home. But in mine, Will, don't you ever swear at her again. And don't tell her to shut up. And stop saying 'For Christ's sake, Cheryl.'"

"Dad—my life is going to be some kind of hell."

"I bet it might," Bill said in a speculative tone. "It well might." Just then the sign-bearers came up to them. One said, "Good afternoon, Mr. Benty," to Bill. The other of them said in a very pleasant tone, "There must be some other way human beings can make money besides on contracts for spreading nerve diseases that cause victims five or six hours of agony," and they made to pass on.

"Off the lawn, friends," Bill said levelly. "Sidewalk's public, lawn's private."

"Agony is another word for torture," the first protester said, but they immediately crossed the street.

As Bill and Will came back to the house, Bill said in a low voice, "Go for the pleasant moments, son. Whenever you can."

All the difficult conversations took place that could take place: all the permanent grievances—Will's and Cheryl's unhappiness—were hinted at. People felt that they had expressed themselves a little. By the end of the day, they felt gritty and exhausted.

A blessed week passed, and now the baptism party was going off well. The caterers had come, with their white Styrofoam trays. They set out sauces and laid the champagne crooked into its pails of ice. They dropped the lobsters into boiling water. There was lemon mayonnaise and drawn butter, a platter of dark-meat turkey—damper, better than white meat, Lois Benty and the caterers agreed. It is true that as she made her way around the Bentys' dining room table, loading her plate, Doreen Oppedahl whispered to her husband, "It'd never occur to me, I can tell you, to serve dark meat on a company occasion," and Merv whispered back, "No, it never *would* occur to you!" but his tone wasn't malicious. He had spotted the Scotch on the sideboard. That Bill Benty might be pompous, but at least he was as good as his word, and Merv wasn't going to be stuck with that dumb champagne, which tasted like Seven-Up with aspirin. An oblong of pinewood lay piled with ham so thin it wrinkled in waves. The caterers had set parsley here and there, and sprayed mist over everything; they set one tiny chip of ice on each butter pat. "Those caterers just left that chutney preserve that Mrs. Wells brought right in its mason jar," Doreen whispered to Merv. He smiled and whispered, "Shut up, Doreen." She whispered back, "If you get drunk at this party, I will never forgive you."

When all the relations and friends had gathered into the living room, Bill Benty tinkled a glass and asked them to drink to his grandchild. After that, people glanced about, weighing places to sit.

Then the one thing that neither the host nor the hostess had foreseen happened: no one sat in the little groupings Lois had arranged. Nor did people pull up chairs to what free space there was at the dining room table. They gravitated to the messy screened porch off the kitchen. The caterers obligingly swept away all their trays and used foil. People dragged out dining room chairs; other people camped on the old wooden chairs already out there.

The morning's breeze had held. Some of it worked through the gritty screens. People relaxed and felt cheerful. They kept passing the baby about, not letting any one relation get to hold her for too long. Father Geoffrey kept boring people by remarking that it was the most pleasant baptism he could remember. Suddenly Lois Benty pointed across at Chad's and Jodi's plates. "Don't *tell* me you two aren't eating the lobster!" she screamed. "Lobster is not meat, you know!"

Both Chad and Jodi gave the smile that experienced vegetarians keep ready for arrogant carnivores. "Well, you see," Jodi said with mock shyness, "we asked the caterers—you see, we did ask. The lobsters weren't stunned first!"

Father Geoffrey said pleasantly, "And delicious they are, too. I've never tasted better."

Jodi said, "They were dropped in alive, you see ... So it's a question of their agony." Then Jodi said in a hurried, louder voice, "Mrs. Benty, please don't worry about us! We always bring our own food, so we're all set." She reached into her back jeans pocket and brought out two plastic bags of cous-cous and sunflower seeds. "We are more than O.K.," she said.

Lois asked people if she could bring them another touch of this or that— the ham, at least? she said, smiling at Mrs. Oppedahl.

"Oh, no!" cried Mrs. Oppedahl. "I've eaten so much! I'd get fat!"

By now Merv had had three quick, life-restoring glasses of Scotch. For once he felt as urbane and witty as Bill Benty, even if he wasn't the boss of a chemical industry.

"Fat!" he shouted. "Afraid you'll get fat! Don't worry! I like a woman fat enough so I can find her in bed!"

He looked around with bright eyes—but there was a pause. Then Bill Benty said in a hearty tone, "Oh, *good* man, Oppedahl! *Good* man!"

Quickly, the baby's great-aunt said to Jodi Plathe, "Those little bags look so interesting! Could you explain what's in them? Is that something we should all be eating?"

Bill said, "Go ahead, Jodi. Convert her. That's what I call a challenge. If you can get her to set down that plate of lobster and eat bulgur wheat instead, you've got something there, Jodi!"

Jodi gave him a look and then said, "No, you tell *me* something, Ms. Wells. I was wondering, why were you crying at the baptism this morning? Somebody said you never went to church at all, and yet ... I was just wondering."

"Oh," Lois Benty said, getting set to dilute any argument, "I bet you mean during the chrism."

Molly Wells happened to be holding the baby at that moment. Above its dreaming face, hers looked especially tired and conscious. "My dear," she said, "that is a long story. I just know you don't want to hear it."

"Let's have the story, lady," Mr. Oppedahl said. "My wife is always so afraid that I'll tell a story—but the way I look at it is, people like a story. You can always ask 'em, do they mind a little story? And if they don't say no, the way I look at it is, it's O.K. to tell it. So go right ahead. Or I could tell one, if you're too shy."

"Never mind!" cried Bill. "Out with it, Molly!"

Father Geoffrey said gently, "I know I for one would surely like to hear it!"

Molly Wells said, "I have to confess I was mostly daydreaming along through the service, thinking of one thing and another. I never liked church. Unlike Bill here—Bill's my first cousin, you might not know—I was raised in the country, and my dream—my one and my *only* dream—was to get out of the country and marry a prince and live happily ever after.

"The only way I could think to escape at seventeen was to go to Bible camp. So I went—and there, by my great good luck, I met another would-be escaper, Jamie Wells. We cut all the outdoors classes and then used those same places where the classes met to sit and walk together when no one was there. We met in the canoe shed. We sat on the dock near the bin of blue and white hats, depending on how well you swam. We met in the chapel, even, during off times. Wherever we were, we were in love all the time. I recall Jamie said to me, 'There is nothing inside me that wants to go back to the old life, Molly. Is there anything inside you that wants to go back to the old life?' There wasn't, so we ran away. Away meant to stay with his parents and sister, who were at a resort in the Blue Ridge Mountains that summer. We told them we wanted to be married, and they were kind to us. We married, and we lived in love for thirty years.

"It was so pleasant—in the little ways as well as the big ones. Jamie found a hilltop that looked over the valley and across to two mountains—Pisgah and The Rat. He told the workmen how to cut down the laurels and dogwoods and just enough of the armored pine so that you couldn't see the mill down in the valley but you had a clear view to the mountains. We spent hours, hours every day, sitting on our stone terrace. We even had Amos and George bring breakfast out there. I remember best sitting out there in March, when the woods were unleafed except for the horizontal boughs of dogwood everywhere! They looked so unlikely, so vulnerable, out there among all that mountain scrub! The ravines were full of red clay, and the sound of the hounds baying and baying, worrying some rabbit all the time. I remember how we always made a point of taking walks in late afternoon, and I would never stop feeling dazzled by the shards of mica everywhere.

And Jamie did have the most wonderful way of putting things. He said mica was bits left over from the first world, back when it was made of pure crystal, when it was made of unbroken love, before God made it over again with clay and trees, ravines, and dogs. I recall when he said that kind of thing my heart used to grow and grow.

"Nothing interrupted us. Now, Jamie's sister, Harriet Jean, always wanted me to do social work for her, but she forgave me when she saw I wasn't going to do it. I expect she understood right off from the very first that I loved her brother, and all a maiden lady really wants from a sister-in-law is that she should really love her brother. We three got along very well. One day, on Amos and George's day off, we had a copperhead on the terrace and Harriet Jean was over there in a flash, and she shot its head right off with her twenty-gauge. She was so good about it, too: I remember she told us very clearly, 'I want you and Jamie to just turn your back now,' and she swept up its head and slung its body over the dustpan handle and carried it off somewhere. She had a good many projects with the black people, and she would have liked me to help her with those ... but after a while she said to me, 'Molly, I see that you have your hands full with that man, and I mean to stop pestering at you,' and she was good as her word. Different occasions came and went—the Vietnam War, I certainly remember that clear as clear. It was in the paper, and when Amos and George came out with the breakfast trays and brought that paper, Jamie said, 'There is a time when a country is in a kind of death agony, the way a person could be,' and I felt a burst of love for him then, too. No one in my family could ever observe and think that clearly."

At this point, Mr. Oppedahl said in a loud but respectful voice, "I didn't just get what you said he did for a living."

Molly Wells said, "Oh, that. He had a private income—that whole family did. Of course, he had an office he had to keep to tend his interests with—but it was private income." She shifted the baby, and seemed to rearrange herself a little as she said that. It didn't invite further comment.

She took up her story. "Everything went along all those years, except of course we just wept uncontrollably when George died, and Amos never was so springy serving us after that.

"Then one day we found out that Jamie had inoperable cancer of the lung."

There was a little pause after she said that. They could all hear the footsteps of people on the sidewalk, outside. The wind had cooled a little.

"They wanted to do radiation on Jamie, because there were some lung cancer cells in his brain. Well, so we had the radiation treatment. I drove Jamie all the way to Asheville for that, twice a week. It was a very hard time for us: he was often sick. When he wasn't actually sick, he felt sick.

"They managed to kill those lung cells in his brain, and gradually, after many months, he died, but not of brain cancer.

"Well, now," the middle-aged woman said. "Three occasions all came to mind during that baptism service for this beautiful little girl this morning. First, after I had been married not two months, I noticed, the way you gradually get around to noticing everything there is about a man, that the flesh in his upper arm was a little soft, just below the shoulder bulge. I could have expected that, since Jamie just wasn't interested in sports at all and he didn't do any physical work. But still I remember thinking: That bit of softness there will get a little softer all the time, and after twenty years or so it might be very soft and loose from the muscle, the way the upper part of old men's arms are—which kills a woman's feeling just at the moment she notices it. Right away, of course, if it is someone dear to you, you forgive them for that soft upper arm there, for not being young and handsome forever, but still the image of it goes in, and you feel your heart shrink a little. You realize the man will not live forever. Then you love him even better in the next moment, because now—for the first time—you pity him. At least, I felt pity.

"The second occasion is when he was sick having all that radiation. He vomited on our living room floor. It was Sunday evening. We always let Amos go home to his own folks on Sundays, so there wasn't anyone to clean that up—but Harriet Jean was there, and she offered to. Suddenly I remember almost snarling at her—I just bayed at her like a dog. I told her to keep out of it. I would clean up my own husband's mess. Of course she was surprised. She couldn't have been more surprised than I was, though. That night in bed, I went over it carefully, and I realized that the only physical life I had left with Jamie was taking care of him, so his throw-up was a part of my physical life with him. Not lovely—but there it was.

"The last occasion was about a half hour after his death. The hospital people told me I had to leave the room, and I remember I refused. Finally they said I could stay another ten minutes and that was all. Now, you all may know or you may not know that they have their reasons for taking people away from dead bodies. I laid my forehead down on the edge of the bed near Jamie's hip—and then I heard a slight rustling. My mind filled with horror. I lifted my head and looked up to see a slight change in his hand. It had been lying there; now the fist—just the tiniest bit, but I wasn't mistaken—was closing a little. When a person looks back cooly from a distance on a thing like that, you know it is the muscles shrinking or contracting or whatever they do when life has left. To me, though, it was Jamie making the very first move I had ever seen him make in all my life with him in which I had nothing to do with it. He was taking hold of something there—thin air, maybe—but taking hold of it by himself. Now I knew what death was. I stood up and left.

"This morning, in church, I was daydreaming about him again. It's a thing I do. I was not going to mention it to any of you.

"I told you about this because I was so surprised to find how my life was not simple at all: it was all tied up in the flesh, this or that about the flesh. And how is flesh ever safe? So when you took that palm oil," she finished, glancing across at Father Geoffrey, "and pronounced our little Molly here safe—*safe!*—in our Lord Jesus Christ forever ... well, I simply began to cry!"

She sat still a moment and then with her conventional smile looked across at the younger godmother. "Well, you asked the question, and now I have answered you."

In the normal course of things, such a speech would simply bring a family celebration to an absolute stop. People would sit frozen still as crystal for a moment, and then one or another would say, in a forced, light-toned way, "My word, but it's getting late ... Dear, we really must ..." and so forth. But the Benty family were lucky. A simple thing happened: it began to rain finally, the rain people had been wanting all summer. It fell quite swiftly right from the first. It rattled the ivy, and then they could even hear it slamming down on the sidewalks. Footsteps across the avenue picked up and began to run.

They all noticed that odd property of rain: if it has been very dry, the first shower drives the dust upward, so that for a second your nostrils fill with dust.

Then the rain continued so strongly it cleaned the air and made the whole family and their friends feel quiet and tolerant. They felt the classic old refreshment we always hope for in water.

Guides to Reflection

1. What are your reactions to the characters in the story? Are there some you like better than others? Do some seem admirable? Despicable? Pitiable? Foolish? Wise? How do your judgments of the characters affect the way you respond to the baptism and the reception afterwards?

2. Bly tells us of three characters' youthful experiences at summer church camps. Bill Benty remembers scornfully the "sissy, capon death they taught you about at Cass Lake Episcopal Camp" *(Reader, 94)*, contrasting that with the apparently manful death he and his friends imagine inside an overturned canoe. Cheryl Oppedahl Benty had a more positive experience at her camp. Bill reports that Cheryl "told me the first time she ever felt popular, as she put it, was at Lutheran Bible camp, when all the girls discovered she could harmonize to the hymns.... She told me that just that one Lutheran Bible Camp gave her more nourishment—her word—than she'd ever got from her parents" *(Reader, 96)*. And Molly Wells—though she says "I never liked church" *(Reader, 100)*—meets her future husband at church camp and embarks on a 30-year-long happy marriage. What do each of these three church camp stories reveal about each of the characters, particularly about their religious beliefs and their experiences in religious institutions?

3. How do you respond to the various marriages Bly portrays in "After the Baptism"? What seems to characterize these relationships? How do husband and wife relate to each other? Look particularly at the marriages of Bill and Lois Benty, Will and Cheryl Benty, Merv and Doreen Oppedahl, Chad and Jodi Plathe, and Molly and Jamie Wells.

4. Most of "After the Baptism" is told from Bill Benty's point of view; that is, Bly tells the story as though Bill himself were telling it to us. How does Bill's strong, opinionated voice affect your reading of the story? How, for instance, does his attitude toward religion affect your response to the baptism?

5. The story's ending seems very hopeful. The people at the reception momentarily overcome their differences to listen to Molly's story, and the rain comes to wash and refresh a thirsty, dusty world. How closely related to the baptism itself do you find this hopefulness? That is, does Bly seem to base the hopefulness in Molly's storytelling, in the wind and rain, or in the Christian Sacrament of Baptism?

6

Gail Godwin

In a published journal entry from the late 1980s, Gail Godwin recalls a dream in which she is campaigning for public office. When asked in the dream to define her particular political program, she replies straightforwardly, "Constructive sorrow. My platform is constructive sorrow."[1] Her answer provides an insight into one of the central themes of her fiction: the power of suffering, when it is embraced actively and with imagination, to open us to the depth of our lives. This "constructive sorrow" entails, in the first place, an acceptance of the painful circumstances of our own reality: the peculiar fears that beset each us of, the unsatisfied longings, the parts of us that are inevitably broken either by the weight of our human inheritance or by our own actions. But such an acceptance of circumstance is only the beginning. What matters most is what we make of what we are, the way we play the hand that fate or providence has dealt us.

Godwin typically illustrates this playing of fate's hand by writing about writers, men (or more often, women) who take the script of their experience and then turn it into art. The trick here is to accept the limits and constraints of life precisely as the source of liberation, to see that the closed door is none other than the way out. Such a vision may be most apparent in the creative process of fiction writers, people who use stories to free their imaginations from life's dead ends and, in doing so, free their readers as well.

But this art of "revision," of looking again and seeing more, is by no means limited to artists. Every person has both an inherited script and the power to revise it, a given history and the freedom to see it and tell it anew. The path of wisdom, therefore, consists in being able to see things as they are and then to imagine them otherwise. Or, as one character puts it in Godwin's most recent novel, *The Good Husband*, "We can't grow up, we can't escape our tormentors, we can't be *free*, until we can express ourselves well enough to be heard by others.... Only then can we tell our story. And only by convincingly telling our story can each of us do our bit to help the world grow up."[2]

In Godwin's nine novels and two collections of short fiction, "telling our story" is explored largely from a psychological point of view. But in her more recent work—*A Southern Family* (1987), *The Good Husband* (1994), and most explicitly, *Father Melancholy's Daughter* (1991)—she has become more openly theological, offering the reader a specifically Christian vision of what it might mean to recognize the design of one's own being.

In *Father Melancholy's Daughter*, for instance, this means watching Margaret Gower grow up and away from the painful drama of her parents' lives in order to tell her own story. There is more at work here, however, than the feminist self-fashioning that Godwin has explored in earlier works, for Margaret comes to understand the unique particularities of her own experience in the light of Christ. Her personal story is grounded in a religious history that is also shared, to one degree or another, not only with her father but with most of the novel's other characters. Here Christianity is common property.

Indeed, narrative time in the novel unfolds within the liturgical year and is centered on Good Friday. Holy Week sermons are written and preached; a crucifix is vandalized and reconsecrated; conversations about the faith are carried on in jest and earnest; and psychological problems are discussed within the context of Christ's passion, death, and resurrection. One way of seeing *Father Melancholy's Daughter* is as Godwin's version of the "church novel" familiar in British fiction—Anthony Trollope or Barbara Pym transplanted to small town Virginia. And yet having made this connection, one sees how much more serious and theological Godwin is about depicting her characters' attempts to live their faith amid their foibles, how they come to discover God's grace in the most unlikely of circumstances.

If a more open involvement with Christian material can be said to indicate a new turn in Godwin's writing, it may in fact represent a return to her earliest inspiration. "An Intermediate Stop," with its clergyman protagonist and overt theological interests, grows out of the author's own experience as a student in North Carolina, when a Scottish Presbyterian minister conducted a religious retreat at her college.[3] Years later, when working in London and taking a course at the City Literary Institute, Godwin turned that visit into fiction. In a journal entry she reveals its first title ("The Illuminated Moment—and Revisions") and makes the following observations: "The vicar is a young man, just thirty-one last June—physical description—eyes which have seen God—focus on his personality at the beginning. Metaphor for artist after first book!"[4] The eventual story was the piece she submitted successfully for admission to the Writer's Workshop at the University of Iowa. It was also her first fiction to be accepted for publication and, under its current title, one of 15 stories later included in *Dream Children* (1976).

The academic setting of "An Intermediate Stop," together with its comic exposure of the ups and downs experienced by a writer on the lecture circuit, link this early story to *The Good Husband,* one of whose major characters, Hugo Henry, regularly leaves Aurelia College to speak (with more or less success) about his own craft as a novelist. The Reverend Lewis in "An Intermediate Stop," however, is not a professional writer. He is a country priest, old beyond his 31 years, who has left behind his centuries-old English vicarage for a North American book tour. His 15th stop, and the last before his return home, is a tiny Episcopal women's college in the deep South.

Lewis is stupefied by the heat, exhausted by the perpetual demands of small talk, and at a loss over how to make any sense out of his prepared remarks. What makes poignant these standard occupational hazards of any author on the road is that the priest's material—the book that his publisher has presumptuously entitled *My Interview with God*—has in effect deserted him. The vision that he initially "stumbled upon" outside the window of his study is gone without a trace, and with it the "Illumination" that at one time had seemed to offer a theological breakthrough for the twentieth century. He can distinctly remember the physical setting of his vision ("a memory of wet green grass, a tree, the sky as it had been, soft pearl, unblemished"), but there is nothing else. All that remains is the sense of a lost "it," a blankly interrogative "what?", a divine subject unwilling to be "interviewed" by any mortal.

Tossing on his bed the night before his lecture, Lewis asks himself a question that goes to the heart not only of Godwin's story but of any attempt to capture and domesticate the experience of God: "Can a fleeting vision be seized by the tail, made to perform again and again to circus music?" *(Reader, 116).* The answer, of course, is no. God is not (to recall the Aslan of C. S. Lewis's *Chronicles of Narnia)* "a tame lion." Nor can we ever enjoy a vision of the kingdom for more than a moment. All human constructs are only place holders for a Spirit that blows where it listeth; or, as the Reverend Lewis puts it, they are only a commemorative coin or "tribute" of treasure that simply cannot be minted.

Nonetheless, the lecturer is, in fact, able to say something. But rather than presenting his audience with "a third-hand rendition of a faded illumination," he gives them instead a picture of his own world: a description of the vicarage garden in which he saw whatever it was he saw; an earthly vision of places not entirely unlike their own; a part of himself. No longer an expert on divinity talking down to his provincial audience, he makes "face to face" contact with them. No longer the stranger from abroad, he finds that by sharing of his own life with his audience "they were with him" *(Reader, 118)*. Such an experience hardly qualifies as an interview with God. What it offers, however, is another glimpse into the kingdom.

Peter S. Hawkins

Notes

1. Gail Godwin, "Journals: 1982-1987," *Antaeus,* no. 61 (Autumn 1988): 195.

2. Gail Godwin, *The Good Husband* (New York: Ballantine Books, 1994), 353.

3. Jane Hill, *Gail Godwin* (New York: Twayne Publishers, 1992), 7.

4. Gail Godwin, "Keeping Track," *Ariadne's Thread: A Collection of Contemporary Women's Journals,* ed. Lyn Lifshin (New York: Harper, 1982), 79.

An Intermediate Stop

The vicar, just turned thirty-one, had moved quietly through his twenties engrossed in the somewhat awesome implications of his calling. In the last year of what he now referred to nostalgically as his decade of contemplation, he had stumbled upon a vision in the same natural way he'd often taken walks in the gentle mist of his countryside and come suddenly upon the form of another person and greeted him. He was astonished, then grateful. He had actually wept. Afterward he was exhausted. Days went by before he could bring himself to record it, warily and wonderingly, first for himself and then to bear witness to others. Even as he wrote, he felt the memory of it, the way the pure thing had been, slipping away. Nevertheless, he felt he must preserve what be could.

Somewhere between the final scribbled word of the original manuscript and the dismay with which he now (aboard a Dixie Airways turboprop flying above red flatland's in the southern United States) regarded the picture of himself on the religion page of *Time* magazine, his tenuous visitor had fled him altogether. The vicar was left with a much-altered life, hopping around an international circuit of lecture tours (the bishop was more than pleased) that took him further and further from the auspicious state of mind which had generated that important breakthrough.

Exhibiting for his benefit a set of flawless American teeth, the stewardess now told him to be sure and fasten his seat belt. "Bayult," she pronounced it. Seat bayult. The trembly old turboprop nosed down toward a country airfield shimmering in the heat, and the captain's disembodied voice welcomed them all to Tri-City Airport, naming the cities and towns that it served, including one called Amity where the vicar was to address a small Episcopal college for women. "Present temperature is ninety-six degrees," said the captain mischievously, as though he himself might be responsible. A groan went up across the aisle, from several businessmen traveling together, wearing transparent short-sleeved shirts and carrying jackets made of a weightless-looking material. It was the middle of September and Lewis had brought only one suit for his three-week lecture tour: a dark flannel worsted, perfect for English Septembers.

He thanked his hostess and, still vibrating to the thrum of the rickety flight, descended shaky metal stairs into the handshake of a fat gentleman who shook his hand with prolonged zest.

"Reverend Lewis, sir, it's an honor, a real honor. I'm Baxter Stikeleather, president of Earle College. How was the weather down there in New Orleans—hotter than here, I'll bet."

"How do you do, Doctor. No, actually it seemed ... not quite so hot."

"Aw, that's 'cause they've got the Gulf Coast sitting right there under their noses, that's why," said the other. Having thus contributed to the defense of his state's climate, he whipped out a huge white handkerchief and beat at his large and genial face, which was slick with perspiration.

They proceeded to the airport terminal, where Stikeleather pounced on Lewis's suitcase as though it contained the Grail and led the way to the parking lot. "The girls sure have looked forward to you coming, Reverend."

"Thank you." Lewis climbed into a roomy estate wagon whose doors bore in hand-lettered Gothic script *"Earle College for Women, founded 1889."* Stikeleather arranged his sphere of a belly comfortably behind the steering wheel. The vicar was going over in his mind what he'd lost just this morning in the New Orleans lecture: ("Getting further is not leaving the world. It is discarding assumptions, thus seeing for the first time what is already there. ...") *What* was already there? What could he have meant? Once these words had connected him to an image, but that image was gone. He had continued glibly on this morning, as though he assumed everyone else knew what was already there, even if he didn't anymore. Perhaps they did know; they seemed to know. Discussing his book with people these past few weeks, he'd had the distinct feeling that they'd tapped a dimension in it that was denied to him, its author.

"... I haven't read it yet," Stikeleather was saying, "but I sure have read a lot about it. I've got my copy, though. I'm looking forward to really immersing myself in it once the semester gets started. What a catchy title. *My Interview with God.* And from what I've heard, it was, wasn't it? Did you think up the title yourself?"

"No," Lewis said uncomfortably. "No, I shan't claim that little accomplishment."

Oh, well," Stikeleather reassured him, "you wrote the book. That's what counts." He stuck the vicar amiably between his shoulder blades and the estate wagon belched from the parking lot in a flourish of flying gravel. "Do you like music?"

"Yes, very much," replied Lewis, puzzled.

"Coming up," the president said, fiddling with knobs on the dashboard. The moving vehicle resounded at once with a sportive melody that made

Stikeleather tap his foot on the carpeted floorboard. "Total Sound," be said.

"It's very nice," said Lewis. ("Matthew's familiar Chapter 6 seems at first to deal with separate subjects. It begins by talking about men who pray loudly in public rather than shut up in their own rooms, and goes on to discuss the impossibility of serving both God and Mammon. But if we look at God as Cause, or Source, and Mammon as certain outward effects, we begin to see a relation. Effects are but the reflection of something that emanates from one's own relationship with the Source. If that relationship is good—'If thine eye be single'—the effect will be full of light; if evil, full of darkness. But any deliberate intention of an effect, casting first towards Mammon with no relevance to the Source, will destroy the possibility of producing a worthwhile one. 'Every circle has its centre / Where the truth is made and meant,' and no good effect can come from focusing on peripheries.") He'd preached that sermon once, in the quiet days before the Illumination and the wretched fame that followed from his poor attempt to deter its passing.

"I went uptown," Stikeleather said, "and bought up all the copies I could find. What I was thinking, after your talk tomorrow morning, you might autograph them. I'll give each trustee one and keep two in our library. I hope you'll write a little something in mine, as well."

"I'd be delighted," Lewis said, charmed by his host's refreshing simplicity. Pale Dr. Harkins, two weeks ago at Yale: walking Lewis down the path to the Divinity School among first fallen leaves, he said, "You seem to be the first person inside organized religion—that is, with the exception of Teilhard (naturally)—to reconcile with success the old symbols and the needs of our present ontology. I have often thought our situation today theologically, is what the *I Ching* would call Ming I (the darkening of the light); we needed your sort of Glossary to light the way again." A Jewish boy at Columbia wedged his way under Lewis's big black umbrella and, biting his nails, hurried out with him to the taxi waiting to speed the vicar to LaGuardia for the Chicago flight. (What was his major? Something wild, eclectic, like Serbo-Croatian poetry.) He said, "But listen, Father, haven't you in an extremely subtle way, acceptable to modern intellectuals, simply reaffirmed the Bible stories?" "I ... I intended to *affirm*, by way of modern myths, the same truths cloaked in the ancient myths, many of which we can no longer find acceptable. I hoped to contain that Truth which remains always the same within the parallels of the old and new myths ... if you see what I mean." "Sure, Father. God between the lines." In San Francisco, he dined one night atop the city with a Unitarian minister his own age who had published an article on the six stages of LSD. The minister found Lewis's famous Interview directly comparable to stage 3 of the Trip "during which there's a

sudden meaningful convergence of conceptual ideas and especially meaningful combinations in the world are seen for the first time." Over brandy,
the minister offered to assist Lewis in reaching stage 6, "uniform white
light," if he would care to accompany him back to his home. But Lewis had
a morning lecture at Berkeley and declined the offer.

"I declare, I feel a whole lot better now, Reverend. There is nothing more
necessary, to my way of thinking, than air-conditioning in your automobile.
The trustees hemmed and hawed till I finally told them point-blank: I per-
sonally cannot drive the school station wagon until it is air-conditioned. I
can't go picking up people in the name of the college and be sweating all
over the place."

"It's jolly nice," agreed Lewis, feeling better himself. He looked out of
the closed window at a baked clay landscape. A group of prisoners whose
striped uniforms were covered with reddish dust labored desultorily in the
terrible heat, monitored by a man carrying a gun. He remembered the quiet
rainy garden in Sussex, outside the vicarage study window—how, looking
out at this scene one totally relaxed moment after many hours of thought,
he had seen suddenly beyond it into a larger, bolder kingdom. He had seen
… He tried now to see it again, focusing intently on a memory of wet green
grass, a tree, the sky as it had been, soft pearl, unblemished; he pushed hard
at grass, tree, sky, so hard they fell away, leaving him with his own frowning
reflection upon the closed window of the air-conditioned station wagon.

"… Unfortunate thing. My wife has the flu; she comes down with it every
fall. I thought it would be risky to put you up at our house, so I asked Mrs.
Grimes, our school nurse, to fix up a private room in the infirmary for you.
Parents of our girls often stay there when the hotel uptown is full. I hope
you aren't offended."

"Not at all," said Lewis, "It will be a change from those motels with the
huge TVs and the paper seals over the lavatories."

Stikeleather whooped with appreciation over this description until Lewis
began to find it rather funny and started laughing himself.

At dinner he soon became quite sure that no faculty member had actually
read his book. Nevertheless, he was the undisputed focus of solicitude.
Wedged between Miss Lillian Bell, who taught history and social sciences,
and Miss Evangeline Lacy (American literature, English literature, and
needlework), he was plied from either side with compliments, respect, and
much affectionate passing back and forth of crusty fried chicken and buttermilk biscuits. He felt like a young nephew who has succeeded in the outside world and comes home to coast for a time in the undemanding company
of doting maiden aunts to whom his stomach is more important than his
achievements.

Miss Bell was the aggressor of the two women. Fast-talking and flirtatious, with leathery, crinkled skin and pierced ears, she played self-consciously with a tiny ceramic tomato bobbling from her earlobe. "We've all looked forward to this so much, Reverend," she said. "Most of our girls have never met an Englishman, let alone an English vicar."

"It is such a pleasure listening to your accent," crooned Miss Lacy, who had possibly been a raving beauty in her youth. Her enormous storm-gray eyes, lashed and lustrous, peered out of her old face from another era and seemed fascinated by all they saw.

"I'm going to tell you something that will surprise you, Reverend," said Lillian Bell. "Both my father and my grandfather were Episcopal ministers. You're not just saying in your book, like some are today, that God is just energy, are you?"

"Certainly not just energy," he assured her, biting into a second chicken leg and munching busily, while framing his words for further explication. He was tired beyond thought. His eyes ached when he swiveled them to note that tables full of girls openly studied him. Dr. Stikeleather had gone home to make dinner for the sick wife, leaving him the only man in the dining room. He felt suddenly exhausted by explanations of something he no longer called his own. The darkening of *his* light, he felt, had reached its winter solstice. He clutched at a straw, the only thing left to him in explaining himself to this good woman: a quote from one of his reviewers. He said, "The book is, well, notes towards a new consciousness which reaches beyond known systems of theology."

Miss Bell's face closed down on him. "Are you a God-is-dead man?" she asked coldly.

"No, no!" he shouted, without meaning to. All conversation stopped. All eyes were riveted on the vicar. In a near whisper, he amended, "In my book, I try to offer a series of concepts through which persons without your fortunate religious upbringing, Miss Bell, might also have God."

"Oh, of course," said she, relieved. "I've been saying the same thing myself for years. It's our duty to share with the less fortunate. Will you have another buttermilk biscuit, Reverend?"

After dinner there was, it seemed, a coffee hour to be held in his honor. "You'll have a chance to meet our girls," said Miss Lacy, "some of them from the finest families in the state. Marguerite Earle is in her second year here."

"The Earle of the college's name?" he inquired politely. A tiny throb had set up a regular rhythm just behind his left temple.

"Dabney Littleton Earle was Marguerite's great-great-great-grandfather," explained Miss Lacy. "He was a wealthy planter and built this place as his home in the late seventeen-hundreds. During the War Between the States, it was given over as a hospital for our wounded. After the war was over, unfortunately, it fell into the hands of the Freedman's Bureau, who used it for their headquarters." Here she sighed sadly and her friend Miss Bell shook her earrings furiously at the outrage. "But in 1889, the Episcopal diocese bought the property and established the college. As a matter of fact, I went here myself, but that was an awfully long time ago."

The coffee hour was in the drawing room. He stood, with a whopping great headache now, backed against a faded brocade curtain, facing a semi-circle of avid ladies; holding his cup and saucer close against his chest like a tiny shield, he accepted their admiration. President Stikeleather entered suddenly. En route to Lewis, he plunged briefly into a cluster of girls long enough to pluck from it the flower of them all. Steering this elegant creature by her elbow, he cruised beaming toward the vicar.

"Reverend Lewis, may I present Miss Marguerite Earle, president of the Earle Student Body," he announced, his voice breaking with pride.

"How do you do?" said Lewis, marveling at the sheer aesthetic value of her. The flaunted English complexion paled beside this girl's pellucid sheen in which morning colors dominated. He counted five such colors in her face: honey, rose, gold, pearl, and Mediterranean blue.

She took Lewis's hand in her cool one and looked up at him with deference. "I have really looked forward to this," she said. "All of us have. Won't you sit down? Let me get you another cup of coffee."

At this gentleness within such beauty, Lewis felt close to tears. Gratefully, he let himself be led to a beige settee. Stikeleather, overflowing with pleasure, stepped over to compensate the semicircle of ladies abandoned by the vicar.

Marguerite returned with his coffee and sat down. "I think it would be wonderful to live in England. Especially the English countryside. When I graduate, if I ever do, and take my trip abroad, I'm going straight to England. I love those people in Jane Austen. So relaxed and witty and tactful with one another. You know something funny, Reverend Lewis? I felt more at home reading her than I sometimes feel in real surroundings."

"I can understand that," he said. "Yours is rather a Jane Austen style. I'm a fan of hers, myself. *Emma* has always been my favorite, however, and you know one can't honestly say she was always tactful. The thing with Miss Bates, for instance, was—Have I said something to upset you?"

"Oh, dear, I've only read *Pride and Prejudice*. We had it in Miss Lacy's class last spring. You must think I'm an idiot." The girl flushed, laced her long fingers together in confusion, and looked perfectly charming.

"Not to worry," he said. "All the better, to have *Emma* ahead of you. You can go back into that world you love without waiting to graduate. But look—a favor for me: remember when you come to Reverend—Reverend—oh, blast, what is his name. You know, Miss Earle, I have forgotten everything but my own name these past few weeks. Well, anyway, when you come to that pompous reverend somebody in *Emma*, don't believe all vicars are like him."

"Oh, whenever I think of an English vicar, I certainly won't think of *him*," she said. She wore some delicate woodsy scent that opened up long-neglected channels in his dry bachelor existence. "Will you tell us about the country homes tomorrow, and the English nobility?"

"Well, certainly if there's time. I mean—if there's time. I've been invited to give my, you know, lecture on the b-book." He paused, amazed. He had not stuttered since his Oxford days, when he'd never quite mastered the knack of smooth conversation with lovely women.

"Oh, I hope there'll be time," she said. "The girls have loads of questions. Where exactly do you live?"

"In a s-small village in Sussex, near the Downs—"

"I declare I hate to disturb you-all, looking so relaxed." Stikeleather stood before the settee. "But there are some who haven't met you yet, Reverend. May I borrow him for just a minute, Marguerite? I want you to meet Miss Julia Bonham, who teaches modern dance, Reverend. He led Lewis away, toward a fulsome lady awaiting them beside the silver service.

Having finally achieved his bed in the infirmary, he couldn't sleep. He fingered the choice of bedside reading left for him by Mrs. Grimes. There was a mint-green *Treasury of Religious Verse*, brand new, with the price $8.95 written in pencil just inside the cover; a choice of Bibles (RSV or King James); and back issues of an inspirational pamphlet called *Forward: Day by Day*. There was a paperback book of very easy crossword puzzles, most of which had been worked in pencil, then erased. Book thoughts led inevitably to consideration of his own 124-page effort, out there in the world, an object in its own right now, separate even from the thing that had inspired it, which was gone. What was that vile vicar's name in the Emma book? Pelham? Stockton? The wife with the brother-in-law in Bristol with his everlasting barouche-landau ... When you began forgetting the villains of literature, you were definitely losing your grip.

He tried different positions: board-straight, scissors-legs, fetal. He clanked around the hospital bed like a lorry full of scrap metal. His bones strummed with phantom vibrations from the turboprop and under the bottom sheet was a waterproof pad that caused his feet to slide. "What a catchy title; did you think it up yourself?" ("What were you thinking of calling it, Mr. Lewis?" over a pint of bitter at the publisher's lunch. "Oh, I don't know.

It's difficult to call it anything. It was what it was, simply: a very fleeting glimpse of God on His own terms, quite apart from all my previous notions of Him. I've said all I was able to say about this, er, glimpse, in my book. Why not just *View from a Sussex Vicarage,* something of the sort?" "Ah, come, Mr. Lewis, let us put our heads together over another pint and see if we can't come up with something more provocative. After all, 'Feed my Lambs' has become today a matter of first winning their appetites, has it not?") 'Every circle has its centre / Where the truth is made and meant,' and no good effects will come from focusing upon peripheries. "We needed your sort of Glossary to light the way again." Going out to LaGuardia in the speeding taxi, through sheets of rain, he saw the most appalling cemetery, miles and miles of dingy graves, chock-a-block.... "Sure, Father, God between the lines." "When You're Out of Schlitz, You're Out of Beer," he was warned again and again on the turnpike. Blessed are the pure in heart, for they shall see ... uniform white light? And then darkness, darkness, darkness, plenty of it. What was that damn vicar's name? Parkins, Sheldon; force it. Can a fleeting vision be seized by the tail, made to perform again and again to circus music? That perfume she was wearing ... The Blessed Henry Suso, after seeing God, was tormented by a deep depression that lasted ten years.... The scent reminded one of spicy green woods, hidden fresh-water springs; he knew so little of women's lore, how they created their effects, yet he was not even old, thirty-one. Was this to be his dry and barren decade, his Dark Night of the Soul? (Mr. Knightley was thirty-seven when he proposed to Emma Woodhouse.) He had been so immersed in his commitment: representative of Christ on earth. Vicar, vicarius: God's deputy. No light matter. He had trod overcarefully, unsure of his right to be there at all. Had his most unsound days, then, been his most profound? Parnham, Parker, Pelton, Felpham, Farnhart, Rockwell, Brockton? Hell. Was there to be no Second Coming? He slept, then, dreamed he and Stikeleather sat under a tree in the vicarage garden, discussing how much it would cost to air-condition the vicarage. Marguerite and her friends, wearing flowing afternoon dresses to their ankles, played a lively game of croquet. Marguerite smashed a red ball CRASH! through his dusty study window, and he was alarmed, but then Stikeleather began laughing, his large belly jiggling up and down, and Lewis, infected, began to laugh, as well, until tears came into his eyes.

At breakfast, there were more of the buttermilk biscuits, which one soaked in a spicy ham gravy called "red-eye." Anxious about giving a lecture that had dried up on him in New Orleans, he ate too many. He signed Miss Bell's copy of *My Interview with God* feeling an impostor.

When he mounted the speaker's platform in the little chapel, everyone applauded him. Eight biscuits soaked in red-eye clumped stubbornly together and refused to digest. He shuffled his pile of note cards, dog-eared from fourteen other lectures, and cleared his throat. He addressed Dr. Stikeleather, who was perspiring lightly in seersucker in the front row, and called every faculty member by name (there were only six). This caused another flurry of delighted clapping. He wished he might repeat the stunt with the girls, but there were too many of them; "charming young ladies" would have to suffice.

"Well, now," he began, flushing, and looking down at the first 4 x 6 note card. One more time, he must give this lecture. He thought of the VC-10 that would depart tonight, with him aboard, for London.

The first note card read:

> a. Unitive life, df. state of transcendent
>   vitality (Underhill)
> b. Luke 14:10
> c. things *seen*

He failed utterly in seeing how these puzzling fragments had ever arranged themselves into an effortless, meaningful opening. Yet here he was; here they were. What, in his totally depleted hour, could he tell them? His feet, it seemed, touched down on the abyss; the light that had been darkening steadily for a year and a half now switched off. And they were waiting, with upturned faces. What to say?

Then he saw Marguerite Earle, his croquet girl, sitting by the window, her bright hair aflame like a burning bush from the morning sun, and he remembered. His Amity muse, a veritable earthly vision, shone before him in her raiments of color with the promise of a rainbow and gave him his topic. Hands folded neatly on her lap, she smiled at him, waiting to hear.

He squared his note cards with a final clack, turned them face down on the rostrum, and said, "The reason I am here with you this morning is because nearly two years ago I was sitting calmly in my vicarage study, looking out on a peaceful rainy afternoon, and, being more or less at one with myself, was admitted—very temporarily—to the presence of God. Afterwards I thought I should preserve the experience by, ah, minting it, in printed words, rather like—well, your Treasury Department distributing the late President Kennedy on silver half-dollars. Only they never for a moment, I am sure, fooled themselves into thinking they were giving away with that coin the essence of the man. It was only a tribute, don't you see, in the same way that my book can only be a tribute to a very special happening. St. Thomas Aquinas once said, long after he'd completed his ponderous *Summa*, 'There are some things that simply cannot be uttered,' after which he serenely folded his hands over his great stomach and spent his last days elevated, they say, in rapturous prayer. Can you not see it, that great portly body floating like a thistle by the Grace of God?"

(There was a short hush during which his audience teetered between respect for a dead saint and amusement at the spectacle of a floating fat one.... Then Stikeleather broke the tie by laughing heartily and they all followed suit.)

"Well, then," Lewis said, a bit breathless, standing naked before them now, a man like any other, no vision standing between them, rather than try and give you a third-hand rendition of a faded illumination, or to go over material which is there for better or for worse in a little green-and-white volume which my publishers call *My Interview with God*, I'd like to return your hospitality to me by taking you briefly into my own world. What shall I show you first? Shall we start with where I live, my vicarage in Sussex, which is five hundred years old?"

Their enthusiastic answer rang out. Marguerite Earle began clapping and they joined her. So he took them first into his study, lined with over four thousand books, many belonging to past vicars dead several hundred years, and warmed even in summer by a fireplace. He led them up narrow circular stairs to his *pièce de résistance*, the loft under the eaves where, in the sixteen-forties, it was rumored that a Royalist vicar had once hidden Charles II from his murderous pursuers. They adored this. He took them to his garden, blushing when he said, "Large enough f-for, um, a game of croquet." In summer, he told them, the Queen's orange-braceleted swans swim upriver and come waddling boldly in the garden at teatime....

He took them on a Cook's tour of London; then, for the benefit of Marguerite, who loved the countryside, he returned them to Sussex Downs for a ramble. It was while lingering there, relaxed and at one with his happy group, in this dreamy country air that he remembered his old friend Mr. Elton, petty vicar of Highbury. Elton, Elton, Elton, of course! He lightened, began the upward trip from his abyss, as though St. Thomas the old dog himself had loaned him a bit of divine buoyancy. Eight buttermilk biscuits melted like hosts in his stomach. Elton! Spouse of Augusta Hawkins for the sum of ten thousand. Hypocrite, flatterer, pompous ass. Lewis had never been so glad to see anyone in his life. His universe expanded as the dark began to fade. He chuckled aloud in the midst of his guided tour. Agreeably, in a body, Earle College chuckled, too, for they were with him.

From *Dream Children* by Gail Godwin. Copyright © 1976 by Gail Godwin. Reprinted by permission of Alfred A. Knopf, Inc. and John Hawkins & Associates, Inc.

Guides to Reflection

1. Godwin's first title for this story was, "The Illumined Moment—and Revisions." The title she later chose, however, is "An Intermediate Stop." Discuss the significance of each.

2. What do we actually know about the "Illumination" that the Reverend Lewis had? Does Godwin ever tell us what the experience was "about"?

3. The decisive role that Margaret Earle seems to play in this story is never quite spelled out. What does she represent for Lewis? What happens to him as a result of making contact with her?

4. Instead of speaking prepared (and often delivered) lecture notes, the Reverend Lewis decides in the end to "wing it." What does he give his audience in lieu of "An Interview with God"?

5. Early in the story Lewis recalls various reactions to his work during earlier stops on his book tour. A divinity school professor talks about his reconciliation of "old symbols" and "our present ontology"; a Columbia University student sums up his efforts as "God between the lines"; and a Unitarian minister in San Francisco makes connections between Lewis's experience of the divine and the final stage of a six-stage LSD "Trip" (Reader, 111). Discuss what each of these conceptions of the "Interview With God" means. Does Godwin offer them simply as comic instances of audience (mis)understanding?

6. Share with one another your own versions of the vision Lewis "stumbled upon" in his own backyard. What can you say about such experiences of the divine? Where have they led you?

7

Kathleen Norris

In her collection of poems *The Middle of the World* (1981), Kathleen Norris assigns the lyric "Harvest" a special designation; she labels it "For David." Then, she begins the poem starkly:

> We'll never belong.
> The pheasant steps out of a medieval tapestry
> Into South Dakota.[1]

Although Norris elsewhere warns her readers against identifying the speakers of her poems with herself ("The 'I' in a poem is never me," she says in *Dakota*[2]), it is tempting to see in these lines of "Harvest" a sketch of the move Norris and her husband made from New York City to Lemmon, South Dakota, in the mid 1970s. As a child, Norris lived in Virginia, Illinois, and Hawaii. Educated at Bennington College in Vermont, she lived in New York in her twenties, working as an arts administrator and writing poetry. When her grandparents died in 1973, Norris and her husband—New York poet and photographer David Dwyer—agreed to live in their home in South Dakota for a year or two. They planned to use the time to find a buyer for the property and settle the estate.

The few years became many, and the opening lines of "Harvest" suggest how difficult it may be to move from the "medieval tapestry" of New York to the desert landscape of Dakota. The city's tapestry is vibrant, lush, and crowded with figures. Rich in its color and dazzling in its intricacy, its elegant interwoven beauty is easy to see. In "Harvest," while the tapestry image recalls New York, there is no such image for South Dakota. It has as yet only a name, not any character or dimension. Lacking an image to suggest its qualities, the desert here seems blank, empty, and spare.

In Norris's book *Dakota*, a 1993 collection of essays and prose poems that became a *New York Times* bestseller, the emptiness of the plains fills in, its blankness gains dimension. During the two decades that passed between Norris's move to Lemmon and the publication of *Dakota*, the prairie offered up its own intricacies—and even images—to her. In *Dakota* Norris says, "the eye learns to appreciate slight variations, the possibilities inherent in emptiness" *(Reader, 124)*. Her essays in the book contain lists of plants, catalogs of animals, descriptions of vistas—all suggesting the lushness of the "small things" *(Reader, 124)*. Nature offers and Norris learns to see in the once impermeable landscape.

Norris becomes an acute observer of social and political realities on the Plains as well. The early chapters in Dakota concern issues such as the economic depression of the 1980s, the inertia of small towns, agriculture, tourism, and nuclear missiles. Toward the middle of the book, she begins to examine in detail the subject promised by her subtitle: "A Spiritual Geography." Dakota, Norris tells us in its first pages, has been:

> the place where I've wrestled my story out of the circumstances of landscape and inheritance. The word 'geography' derives from the Greek words for earth and writing, and writing about Dakota has been my means of understanding that inheritance and reclaiming what is holy in it.[3]

Norris's move to Dakota, then, became for her a "religious pilgrimage."[4] Living on the Plains stimulated her to reexamine her assumptions about religion and spirituality:

> Like many Americans of my baby boom generation, I had thought that religion was a constraint that I had overcome by dint of reason, learning, artistic creativity, sexual liberation. Church was for little kids or grandmas, a small-town phenomenon that one grew out of or left behind.[5]

In South Dakota, Norris began attending her grandmother's Presbyterian church, made friends with the town's ministers (Lemmon is so small, "the poets and ministers have to hang out together"[6]), and became associated with a Benedictine monastery. What Norris learned on her "pilgrimage" changed her:

> As it turns out, the Plains have been essential not only for my growth as a writer, they have formed me spiritually. I would even say they have made me a human being.[7]

The marks of this change in Norris are apparent in the wealth of images she uses to describe Dakota in the book. The Plains are an "inland ocean,"[8] a "vast ocean of prairie."[9] Dakota is like Egypt and Cappadocia, where monasteries were first established in the fourth century. And, more daringly:

> The beauty of the Plains is like that of an icon; it does not give an inch to sentiment or romance. The flow of the land, with its odd twists and buttes, is like the flow of Gregorian chant that rises and falls beyond melody, beyond reason or human expectation, but perfectly. *(Reader, 125)*

These images reveal how the Plains have lost their blankness for Norris, even how they can become a threshold to another world altogether:

> Maybe seeing the Plains is like seeing an icon; what seems stern and almost empty is merely open, a door into some simple and holy state. *(Reader, 125)*

The variety in these images—ocean, Cappadocia, icon, chant, door—suggests the depth of Norris's encounter with the Plains and the direction of the pilgrimage she undertakes there.

In *Dakota*, as the emptiness of the Plains fills in with a tapestry of images, Norris uses a mixture of literary genres to tell the story of her pilgrimage. Some chapters in *Dakota*, such as "Getting to Hope," are essays; some, such as "Seeing," are reflections or meditations; and some, such as "Weather Report: August 9," are prose poems. Each genre offers a different perspective on Dakota and Norris's spiritual geography:

- In the essays, she explores ideas. Multiculturalism, time, the nature of church bureaucracies, smallness, and contemporary attitudes toward death all mark "Getting to Hope."
- In the meditations, she presents parables and descriptions. Lists of plants and animals alternate in "Seeing," for instance, with a "Plains fever" *(Reader, 125)* love story, pointed quotations, and an account of a Native American drum ceremony.
- In the prose poems, some of which appear as poems in her *Little Girls in Church* (1995), Norris accents her prose with the emotional depth and suggestiveness of lyric poetry.

Together, the essays, parables, descriptions, and prose poems chart Norris's rich and intricate spiritual geography.

At the end of "Harvest," Norris asks:

> What will anyone
> Make of us? Two,
> Childless,
> Figures in a field?[10]

Dakota is the story of what Dakota made of Norris, and what Norris made of Dakota. On the book's opening page, Norris tells us: "The High Plains, the beginning of the desert West, often act as a crucible for those who inhabit them. Like Jacob's angel, the region requires that you wrestle with it before it bestows a blessing."[11]; and on its closing page, she reports the wisdom of a monk: "You have only to let the place happen to you."[12] *Dakota* is Norris's account of the landscape's happening and her wrestling as she becomes a spiritual cartographer on the Plains.

Paula J. Carlson

Notes

1. Kathleen Norris, *The Middle of the World* (Pittsburgh: University of Pittsburgh Press, 1981), 18.

2. Kathleen Norris, *Dakota: A Spiritual Geography* (New York: Ticknor & Fields, 1993), 171.

3. *Dakota*, 2.

4. *Dakota*, 93.

5. *Dakota*, 97.

6. *Dakota*, 105.

7. *Dakota*, 11.

8. *Dakota*, 145.

9. *Dakota*, 153.

10. *The Middle of the World*, 18.

11. *Dakota*, 1.

12. *Dakota*, 220.

Seeing

The midwestern landscape is abstract, and our response to
the geology of the region might be similar to our response
to the contemporary walls of paint in museums.
We are forced to live in our eye.
—MICHAEL MARTONE

Abba Bessarion, at the point of death, said, "The monk
ought to be like the Cherubim and the Seraphim: all eye."
—*The Desert Christian*

Once, when I was describing to a friend from Syracuse, New York, a place on the plains that I love, a ridge above a glacial moraine with a view of almost fifty miles, she asked, "But what is there to see?"

The answer, of course, is nothing. Land, sky, and the everchanging light. Except for a few signs of human presence—power and telephone lines, an occasional farm building, the glint of a paved road in the distance—it's like looking at the ocean.

The landscape of western Dakota is not as abstract as the flats of Kansas, but it presents a similar challenge to the eye that appreciates the vertical definition of mountains or skyscrapers; that defines beauty in terms of the spectacular or the busy: hills, trees, buildings, highways, people. We seem empty by comparison.

Here, the eye learns to appreciate slight variations, the possibilities inherent in emptiness. It sees that the emptiness is full of small things, like grasshoppers in their samurai armor clicking and jumping as you pass. This empty land is full of grasses: sedges, switch grass, needlegrass, wheatgrass. Brome can grow waist-high by early summer. Fields of wheat, rye, oats, barley, flax, alfalfa. Acres of sunflowers brighten the land in summer, their heads alert, expectant. By fall they droop like sad children, waiting patiently for the first frost and harvest.

In spring it is a joy to discover, amid snow and mud and pale, withered grass, the delicate lavender of pasqueflower blooming on a ridge with a southern exposure. There is variety in the emptiness; the most prosaic pasture might contain hundreds of different wildflowers along with sage, yucca, and prairie cactus. Coulees harbor chokecherry, buffalo berry, and goose-berry bushes in their gentle folds, along with groves of silvery cottonwoods and Russian olive. Lone junipers often grow on exposed hillsides.

This seemingly empty land is busy with inhabitants. Low to the ground are bullsnakes, rattlers, mice, gophers, moles, grouse, prairie chickens, and pheasant. Prairie dogs are more noticeable, as they denude the landscape with their villages. Badgers and skunk lumber busily through the grass. Jackrabbits, weasels, and foxes are quicker, but the great runners of the Plains are the coyote, antelope, and deer. Meadowlarks, killdeer, blackbirds, lark buntings, crows, and seagulls dart above the fields, and a large variety of hawks, eagles, and vultures glide above it all, hunting for prey.

Along with the largeness of the visible—too much horizon, too much sky—this land's essential indifference to the human can be unnerving. We had a visitor, a friend from back East who flew into Bismarck and started a two-week visit by photographing the highway on the way to Lemmon; "Look how far you can see!" he kept exclaiming, trying to capture the whole of it in his camera lens. He seemed relieved to find a few trees in town and in our yard, and did not relish going back out into open country.

One night he called a woman friend from a phone booth on Main Street and asked her to marry him. After less than a week, he decided to cut his visit short and get off the Plains. He and his fiancée broke off the engage-ment, mutually and amicably, not long after he got home to Boston. The proposal had been a symptom of "Plains fever."

A person is forced inward by the spareness of what is outward and visi-ble in all this land and sky. The beauty of the Plains is like that of an icon; it does not give an inch to sentiment or romance. The flow of the land, with its odd twists and buttes, is like the flow of Gregorian chant that rises and falls beyond melody, beyond reason or human expectation, but perfectly.

Maybe seeing the Plains is like seeing an icon: what seems stern and almost empty is merely open, a door into some simple and holy state.

Not long ago, at a difficult time in my life, when my husband was recov-ering from surgery, I attended a drum ceremony with a Native American friend. Men and boys gathered around the sacred drum and sang a song to bless it. Their singing was high-pitched, repetitive, solemn, and loud. As they approached the song's end, drumming louder and louder, I realized that the music was also restorative; my two-day headache was gone, my troubles no longer seemed so burdensome.

I wondered how this loud, shrill, holy music, the indigenous song of those who have truly seen the Plains, could be so restful, while the Grego-rian chant that I am just learning to sing can be so quiet, and yet as stirring as any drum. Put it down to ecstasy.

Weather Report: August 9

Some 250,000 motorcyclists converge on Sturgis in the Black Hills, boosting South Dakota's population by more than a third. Some two hundred Benedictine men and women gather in the opposite corner of the state, at a convent on the bluffs of the Missouri River.

It's hard to say which gathering is the more important; both are marked by partying and all manner of prayer.

I cast my lot with the monks and nuns. It matters to know where on earth we are. Yankton. The haze of late summer, complete with gnats. There is the Zen of it: "When you come to a place where you have to go left or right," says Sister Ruth, "go straight ahead."

Getting to Hope

To get to Hope, turn south off U.S. Highway 12 at Keldron, South Dakota. It's easy to miss, as the town is not much more than a gas station and general store with a well-kept house behind it, and a sign announcing that Cammy Varland of Keldron was Miss Teen South Dakota of 1987.

Turn onto the gravel section-line road and look for a wooden map on your right. Built by the Busy Beavers 4-H Club, it has the mysterious yet utilitarian air of the seashell, twine, and bamboo maps that South Sea islanders once made for navigational purposes. The Keldron map consists of wooden slats painted with names and numerical inscriptions. Peterson 8 S 4 E 1 N indicates that you would drive eight miles south, four miles east, and one mile north to find the Peterson ranch.

The small metal sign for Hope (13 S) may or may not be up. The wind pulls it down and it can be a while before someone notices and reattaches it. But you don't need directions; just follow the road south and turn when it turns 90 degrees west, then another 90 degrees south, and then it's just another mile or so.

Ten and a half miles along the road, at the crest of the second hill, you'll be able to see where you're going, a tiny ark in a sea of land that unfolds before you for nearly fifty miles. At night you can see the lights of Isabel, South Dakota, some forty-five miles south, and Bison, about the same distance to the southwest.

The breaks of the Grand River are visible, land crumpled like brown paper. The river itself lies at the base of the steep cliffs it has carved into the prairie, sandstone glinting in the morning sun. *Paha Sunkawakan Sapa,* or Black Horse Butte, is a brooding presence on the horizon south of the river.

You will pass a few modest homes and farm buildings along the way, some in use, others in disrepair. The most recently abandoned, a classic two-story house, has boarded-up windows and an extensive but weed-choked corral. A house abandoned years ago is open to the elements, all its windows and most of its shingles gone. A large shelterbelt, planted in the 1930s, is now a thicket of dead trees. Once the trees are gone the house will lean with the wind until it collapses; but that will be a while.

Like the others who have business in Hope, I know who left; I know why. Every time I pass the abandoned houses I am reminded of them. "Hope Presbyterian Church is located by itself on the South Dakota prairie," is what the church history says. But that doesn't begin to tell it. Hope Church, which fifteen years ago had a membership of 46 is down to 25 today, scattered on ranches for thirty miles around. The loss is due to older farmers retiring and moving to town, and younger farmers leaving the area.

Hope Church is an unassuming frame building that stands in a pasture at the edge of a coulee where ash trees and berry bushes flourish; chokecherry, snowberry, buffalo berry. The place doesn't look like much, even when most of the membership has arrived on Sunday morning, yet it's one of the most successful churches I know. Along with Center School, the one-room schoolhouse that currently serves nine children from Grand Valley, Riverside, and Rolling Green townships in southwest Corson County, Hope Church gives the people who live around it a sense of identity.

"It doesn't matter what religion they are," says one longtime member. "The Lutherans and Catholics tell us that Hope is important to them, too, and becoming more so. We're *the church* in the neighborhood." A former pastor said of Hope Church, "It seemed that whatever was going on, a farm sale or a funeral or wedding, Hope was a part of what happened in that community." A measure of this may be seen at the annual Vacation Bible School for children, which is attended by both Lutheran and Catholic children.

The current church was built by its members in 1961 on the cement foundation of an old barn. But its roots go back to 1916, when people gathered for Sunday worship in the dance halls of the small settlements at White Deer and Glad Valley. "Church wasn't awfully regular in the horse and buggy days," says an older member of Hope, the son of one of the founders. "The ministers at McIntosh or Thunder Hawk were circuit riders then, and it could take them half a day to get down to us." Neither congregation ever had a church building. Until they merged in 1950, one congregation met in a one-room school, and the other in a hall that served as a community center where baby showers, funeral luncheons, wedding dances, and anniversary celebrations are also held.

Hope is well cared for. Both the outhouse and the sanctuary are freshly painted. Two small, attractive stained glass windows depicting a cross in the center of a sunburst and a dove with an olive branch flying over a landscape that resembles the fields around Hope Church were recently added to the south wall behind the pulpit, placed on either side of a handmade cross of varnished wood. The elegantly curved oak pews with carved endpieces are hand-me-downs from a church in Minnesota. A member of Hope drove his grain truck more than three hundred miles to get them.

Hope has a noble and well-used upright piano whose sound reminds me of the honky-tonk pianos in Western movies. But when Carolyn plays her quiet-down music at the beginning of a service, "Shall We Gather at the River" or "Holy, Holy, Holy," she's as effective as a Russian Orthodox deacon striding sternly through a church with censer and bells. We know it's time now to listen, that we will soon take our journey into word and song, and maybe change a little along the way. By the time we're into our first hymn, we know where we are. To paraphrase Isaiah 62, it's a place no longer desolate but delightful.

There is no indoor plumbing at Hope, but the congregation celebrates with food and drink at every opportunity. Once, when I arrived on Sunday, I noticed several popcorn poppers in a back pew. That was for after church, to help everyone get through the annual congregational meeting. Once, Hope gave me a party with homemade cake, coffee and iced tea, and Kool-Aid in big coolers that the men carried into the basement.

In the manner of the other tiny country churches I know (United Tribes in Bismarck and Saint Philip's in Maili, Hawaii) Hope is such a hospitable place that I suspect that no matter who you are or where you come from, you will be made to feel at home. But don't get so comfortable that you underestimate the people around you; don't entertain for a moment the notion that these farmers and ranchers are quaint country folk. Most of them have college degrees, though the figure is down slightly from 85 percent in the mid-1980s, a statistic that startled the pastor, who had last worked in Scranton, Pennsylvania, where 3 percent of her congregation was college educated.

Hope's people read, and they think about what is going on in the world. If you want to know anything about agriculture on a global scale—the cattle market in Argentina or prospects for the wheat crop in Australia—this is the place to ask. As one pastor recently put it, "the thing that makes Hope so vibrant is that the congregation is so alive to the world."

Hope's members take seriously their responsibility as members of the world's diverse and largely poor human race. A few years ago, reasoning that people who raise food (and often have a hard time getting a price for it that covers their expenses) should know more about why so many in the world can't afford to feed themselves, they conducted a study of the politics of hunger. To conclude the study they invited an expert on the subject to come from Chicago to address churchpeople in the area. They also studied the ethical issues of raising animals for food. As ranchers who know the life history and temperament of every cow in their herds, they were dismayed to discover the inroads factory farming had made in American agriculture.

In recent hard times, while Hope's membership declined by nearly half, the amount the church donates for mission has increased every year. It now ranks near the top in per capita giving among Presbyterian churches in the state of South Dakota.

One former pastor said, "It can be astonishing how tiny Hope Church makes you feel so strongly that you're part of a global entity." This is a long tradition at Hope. A rancher whose three daughters spent several years in ecumenical church work in Sydney, Paris, Rome, and Brussels says: "Our girls always knew that the world was bigger than just us. They had cousins who were missionaries in China in the 1950s and 1960s. In those days missionaries got every seventh year off, and they'd stay with us on the ranch. Our children grew up hearing stories about other places."

For this and other reasons pastors find the Hope congregation stimulating to work with. One told me if he could sum them up in one word it would be "appreciative." Another said: "Hope was where I realized how much the members of a rural church actually work as well as worship together. They live supporting each other. We'd spoken of such things at seminary, as an ideal, but this was the first time in twenty years of ministry I'd actually seen it done. It made me realize how vital a small country church can be."

Perhaps it's not surprising that so tiny a rural congregation is not often well served by the larger church of which it is a part. For all their pious talk of "small is beautiful," church bureaucrats, like bureaucrats everywhere, concentrate their attention on places with better demographics; bigger numbers, more power and money. The power of Hope Church and country churches like it is subtle and not easily quantifiable. It's a power derived from smallness and lack of power, a concept the apostle Paul would appreciate, even if the modern church bureaucrats lose sight of it.

In the manner of country people everywhere (and poets also for that matter) the people at Hope tend to be conservators of language. Once, when I found myself staggering through a benediction provided by the denomination that, among other things, invited us to "authenticate the past," I stopped and said, "I'm sorry, but that's ridiculous English." Laughter became our benediction that morning.

Like most small churches in the western Dakotas, Hope must be yoked to another, larger church in order to afford a full-time pastor. When Hope's sister church in Lemmon, thirty miles away, received memorial money to purchase a new Presbyterian hymnal that includes many contemporary hymns and more inclusive language, Hope decided to stay with their 1955 model. Not because its members aren't progressive. It's a relatively youthful congregation, in fact, with nary a fundamentalist bone among them. But the old hymnal works well for them, and many of their standards are not included in the new book: "I Need Thee Every Hour" and "I Love to Tell the Story" (which, not surprisingly, has been a favorite of mine since childhood), and "Nearer, My God, to Thee." That last hymn was a revelation to me when I first came back to church. Like many people, I couldn't think of it without picturing the band on the Titanic in *A Night to Remember*. I was pleased to discover that the hymn is an evocative retelling of the story of Jacob's dream.

As one pastor of Hope, a graduate of Princeton seminary, said to me, "Church intellectuals always want to root out the pietistic hymns, but in a rural area like this those hymns of intimacy are necessary for the spiritual welfare of people who are living at such a distance from each other." He added, "City people want hymns that reassure them that God is at work in the world, but people in the western Dakotas take that for granted."

The conflict between urban and rural theologies is an old one in the Christian church. Back in fourth-century Egypt, the Bishop of Alexandria, at the urging of intellectuals smitten with Greek philosophy, announced as church doctrine that when you pray you must not have any picture of God in your mind. One old monk is reported to have wept, saying, "They have taken away my God, and I have none I can hold now, and know not whom to adore or to address myself." Some monks took to their boats and traveled the Nile to Alexandria, where they rioted in front of the bishop's palace until he recanted. Hope's people have been more quiet about letting the greater Church go its way.

I find it ironic that the new inclusiveness of the official church tends to exclude people as rural as those of Hope. But I may have been spoiled by the company I keep on the prairie, the Benedictine monks and country people, some well educated, some not, who know from their experience that prayer is important, that worship serves a purpose, that God is part of everyday life, and that singing "Nearer My God, to Thee" may be good for a person. It's a rural hymn: it's the rare city person who can imagine sleeping out in the open, a stone for a pillow and a heaven of stars above.

Maybe we're all anachronisms in Dakota, a bunch of hicks, and the fact that the images in many old hymns, images of seed and wheat, planting and reaping, images as old as the human race and as new as the harvest in the fields around Hope Church, really aren't relevant any more. Twenty-five Presbyterian farmers, or a handful of monks for that matter, don't have much to say to the world.

And yet I wonder. I wonder if a church like Hope doesn't teach the world in the way a Monastery does, not by loudly voicing its views but by existing quietly in its own place. I wonder if what Columba Stewart, a contemporary Benedictine, has said about such earthy metaphors, that "the significance of field, vineyard and garden metaphors in biblical and postbiblical texts ... lies beyond their relevance to the agricultural economy of ancient peoples," really means that our urban civilization surpasses such metaphors at its peril. As Stewart says, "these images describe the process of human cultivation," and as such they may be an essential part of being human, and of being religious in a human way.

Does the city, any city, need Hope Church? Does America need people on the land? In the last volume of Ole Rolvaag's *Giants in the Earth* trilogy a country pastor, addressing Norwegian farmers in Dakota who are losing their "old country" ways, and in fact are eager to lose them in order to become good Americans, declares that "a people that has lost its traditions is doomed." He adds:

> If this process of leveling down, of making everybody alike ... is allowed to continue, America is doomed to become the most impoverished land spiritually on the face of the earth; out of our highly praised melting pot will come a dull ... smug complacency, barren of all creative thought ... Soon we will have reached the perfect democracy of barrenness ... Dead will be the hidden life of the heart which is nourished by tradition, the idioms of language, and our attitude to life. It is out of these elements that character grows.

The process of acculturation to American life has traditionally been accelerated in cities; it takes more time for rural people to change. But Rolvaag's pastor is as relevant as the contemporary debate about multiculturalism. "If we're to accomplish anything worthwhile," he says, "we must do it as Norwegians. Otherwise we may meet the same fate as corn in too strong a sun."

I wonder if roles are now reversed, and America's urban majority, native born or not, might be seen as immigrants to a world of asphalt and cement, and what they need more than anything is access to the old ways of being. Access to the spirits of land and of place. The image of a democracy of barrenness rings true when one turns on the television and finds bland programs designed for the widest possible audience, or when one drives a busy freeway or walks through an airport parking garage, places that are no place, where you can't tell by looking if you are in Tulsa or Tacoma, Minneapolis or Memphis.

The sense of place is unavoidable in western Dakota, and maybe that's our gift to the world. Maybe that's why most Americans choose to ignore us. Upward mobility is a virtue in this society; and if we must keep moving on, leaving any place that doesn't pay off, it's better to pretend that place doesn't matter. But Hope Church, south of Keldron, is a real place, a holy place; you know that when you first see it, one small building in a vast land. You know it when you walk in the door. It can't be moved from where it is on the prairie. Physically, yes, but that's beside the point.

Hope's people are traditional people, country people, and they know that the spirits of a place cannot be transported or replaced. They're second-, third-, and fourth-generation Americans who have lived on the land for many years, apart from the mainstream of American culture, which has become more urban with every passing year. Hope's people have become one with their place: this is not romanticism, but truth. You can hear it in the way people speak, referring to their land in the first person: "I'm so dry I'm starting to blow," or "I'm so wet now I'll be a month to seeding."

A pastor who was raised on a farm in Kansas said he thought what made Hope special was that the members were "all, or nearly all, totally dependent on the land." He didn't seem to mind that church attendance got sparse at haying time and at calving, which is a round-the-clock operation for most ranch families; every three hours or so someone must check the pregnant heifers. The fact that this often coincides with brutal spring blizzards doesn't help; newborns can freeze to death in a matter of minutes.

"I spent some time on trail rides with Hope's ranchers," the pastor said, "and also helped at lambing. But they were a bigger help to me than I was to them. To touch the earth, the real earth, once again, restored my soul."

I once heard Martin Broken Leg, a Rosebud Sioux who is an Episcopal priest, address an audience of Lutheran pastors on the subject of bridging the Native American/white culture gap. "Ghosts don't exist in some cultures," he said, adding dismissively, "They think time exists." There was nervous laughter; we knew he had us. Time is real to us in America, time is money. Ghosts are nothing, and place is nothing. But Hope Church claims by its very existence that place is important, that place has meaning in and of itself. You're still in America in the monastery, and in Hope Church—these absurd and holy places—you're still in the modern world. But these places demand that you give up any notion of dominance or control. In these places you wait, and the places mold you.

Hope is small, dying, and beautifully alive. It's tribal in a way, as most of its members are related. But it does not suffer from tribalism, the deadening and often deadly insularity that can cause groups of people to fear or despise anyone who is not like them. I find in Hope many of the graces of a monastery, with stability of place and a surprisingly wide generosity in its hospitality.

It was hospitality that allowed the people at Hope to welcome me as a lay pastor. It was absurd for me to be giving sermons to them, the only person in the room who hadn't been to church in the past twenty years. I had little experience of the Bible apart from childhood memories; no training in either Scripture studies or homiletics. What could I possibly say to these people about scriptures they had been absorbing all their lives?

I did what I could, and my long apprenticeship as a poet served me well. I didn't preach much, in the traditional sense of the word; instead I stayed close to those texts, talking about the stories I found there and how I thought they might resonate with our own stories. And I got some thoughtful and encouraging response. I followed the lectionary for discipline, but got a laugh one Sunday when I mentioned that I'd chosen to ignore the advice I'd found in a guide for pastors, that one shouldn't try to connect the Old Testament, Gospel, and Epistle texts but concentrate instead on one brief passage. I said that telling a poet not to look for connections is like telling a farmer not to look at the rain gauge after a storm.

Preaching sermons was a new and unnerving experience for me, and having the people at Hope to work with was my salvation. They made it easier for me to do in those sermons what I saw I had to do, that is, disclose myself in ways different from those I was used to, hiding behind the comfortable mask of fiction. The "I" in a poem is never me—how could it be? But the "I" in my sermons came closer to home, and that was risky. "That's why we appreciated you," one Hope member told me.

I got to try out my sermons first at Hope, as the Sunday morning service there is at 9:00 A.M. and the one in town is at 11:00 A.M. More than once I finished at Hope by asking, "Can I get away with saying this in town?" Once a woman replied, "That depends on how much faith you have," which was a good answer, as the Gospel text that day was the story of Jesus hollering at his disciples in the middle of a storm, "Why are you so afraid?" The church in town had been through a stormy period a few years back, and my sermon was an attempt to help put those bad times to rest. I knew that if I had misjudged, I would only stir things up again.

I began to find that Hope Church opened doors for me the way that Benedictine monasteries had, and it offered similar surprises. Every time I read the Scriptures aloud in the Sunday service at Hope I became aware of sparks in those texts that I had missed in preparing my sermon, and that was a wonderful experience for a poet to have, as it said much about the power of words to continually astonish and invigorate us, and even to surpass human understanding.

Monks, with their conscious attempt to do the little things peaceably and well—daily things like liturgy or chores, or preparing and serving meals—have a lot in common with the farmers and ranchers of Hope. Both have a down-to-earth realism on the subject of death. Benedict, in a section of his *Rule* entitled "Tools for Good Works," asks monks to "Day by day remind yourself that you are going to die," and I would suggest that this is not necessarily a morbid pursuit. Benedict is correct in terming the awareness of death a tool. It can be humbling when we find ourselves at odds with another person, to remember that both of us will die one day, presumably not at one another's hands. If, as Dr. Johnson said, "the prospect of being hanged in the morning wonderfully concentrates the mind," recalling our mortality can be a healthy realism in an age when we spend so much time, energy, and money denying death.

But maybe denying death is something people need to do. One might even look at a medieval cathedral as an expression of that need. Those buildings, however, were also made for celebrating life with music and art, with the play of light and shadow on stone and colored glass. They are beautiful in ways that modern exercise machines and lifestyles leading to that tofu-in-the-sky are not.

Tofu is still a novelty at Hope; people there obtain their protein from animals they raise on land that is suitable for nothing else. I learned at Hope Church just how profoundly the activities of farming and ranching, working the land and working closely with animals, affect the way people approach matters of life and death. Preaching in both a town and a country church, I found that the hard texts of Advent—texts about waiting, about judgment and last things—were accepted in the country while in town there was already pressure to start celebrating Christmas.

When the great wheel of the lectionary came round to the text in Isaiah that begins, "Comfort ye, comfort ye my people," and reminds us that "all flesh is grass," I preached a sermon at Hope that attempted to address the meaning of Advent in terms of the tangle of pain and joy we feel in preparing for birth and death. The town church had opted for no sermon that day. Instead, we sang Christmas carols and listened to sentimental poems from *Ideals* magazine. That text from Isaiah was read aloud during the service, but its meaning was clouded by cheer. We were busy comforting ourselves and had no wish to be reminded of our mortality.

The difference between the two churches on that Sunday confirmed what

I had begun to suspect: the people of Hope Church were less afraid than the people in town to look into the heart of their pain, a pain they share with many monasteries, which also have a diminishing and aging population. When these people ask, "Who will replace us?" the answer is, "who knows, maybe no one," and it's not easy to live with that truth. The temptation is to deny it or to look for scapegoats. The challenge is to go on living graciously and thankfully, cultivating love. Not sentimental love but true charity, which, as Flannery O'Connor said, "is hard and endures."

The people of Hope live far apart from each other on the land: paradoxically, I suspect this is one reason they seem better at creating community than people in town, better at being together while leaving each other alone, as I once heard the monastic ideal defined. How are we to get along with our neighbor in hard times and good? How can we make relationships that last? Those who live in small rural communities, who come to know their neighbors all too well over the years, know the truth of the words of a sixth-century monk, Dorotheus of Gaza: "The root of all disturbance, if one will go to its source, is that no one will blame himself." When I read those words in a sermon at Hope Church, one old farmer forgot himself; he nodded and said aloud, "That's right." He was assenting to a hard truth, one confirmed by a lifetime of experience.

"All flesh is grass" is a hard truth, too, and it has real meaning for people who grow grass, cut it, bale it, and go out every day in winter to feed it to cows. They watch that grass turning into flesh, knowing that they in turn will eat it as beef. They can't pretend not to know that their flesh, too, is grass. And they know that grass dies, not just in the winter, but in summer's dry heat. "All flesh is grass, and its beauty is as the flower of the field." That image comes alive in the West River of Dakota, and also an image from Psalm 90 that speaks of "grass that springs up in the morning" and "by evening withers and fades."

It's hard for me to imagine Hope Church dying, almost impossible to picture it abandoned or falling into ruins, as human constructions inevitably do. Absurdly, I think of its death the way I think of our sun dying. Eventually, long after anyone is around to see it, the sun will grow redder and perhaps more beautiful before it finally burns out. The Grand River will have turned to ice by then, and Black Horse Butte may be stripped of its skin of grass and soil.

It's absurd, too, that I find a Benedictine monastery and a tiny Presbyterian church in the middle of nowhere to be so absolutely and perfectly complementary. I am not showing due respect to religion as I was taught it: as a matter of the fine points of who's in, who's out, who's what as defined by dogmatic and denominational distinctions. But then, I don't have to. This is the Wild West. Out at Hope, in the summer, bellowing cows at a nearby watering tank sometimes join in the call to worship; one year baby rattlesnakes showed up for Vacation Bible School.

One former minister at Hope who had come from the urban East told me that her strongest memory of Hope Church was of an evening service in July. Standing in the pulpit she could see down the length of the church and out the open door to a large round hay bale catching the last rays of sunlight. "It was dark on one side and pure gold on the other," she said, "and I thought, that's a measure of the wealth here, that will help make things come out right this year."

She also told me that she couldn't imagine what was happening at the first funeral service she conducted for a member of Hope Church when, as people gathered for the graveside service, the men, some kneeling, began studying the open grave. It was early November, and someone explained that they were checking the frost and moisture levels in the ground. They were farmers and ranchers worried about a drought. They were mourners giving a good friend back to the earth. They were people of earth, looking for a sign of hope.

Guides to Reflection

1. Norris describes in "Seeing" how nothing becomes something as soon as she trains her eye on it. Does Norris's description of the desert plains call the landscape to life for you as a reader? Which sections strike you as effective, and why?

2. In "Weather Report: August 9," Norris contrasts a huge gathering of motorcyclists in Sturgis with a smaller one of Benedictines in Yankton. What do you think of her use of such a stark contrast? And what do you make of the advice she passes on from Sister Ruth: "When you come to a place where you have to go left or right ... go straight ahead" (Reader, 126)?

3. Norris finds the particularity of place to be of great importance; but she sees it as lacking in contemporary America, except in remote places like Dakota. Think about the various ways Norris evokes a sense of place in these selections from her book. Do you agree with her that urban and suburban Americans are rootless? What do you think of Norris's sense of loss and even danger in the rootlessness she sees in much of America?

4. In "Getting to Hope," Norris says, "I find it ironic that the new inclusiveness of the official church tends to exclude people as rural as those of Hope" (Reader, 130). The fascination for megachurches, "contemporary" liturgies, and gospel bands among church bureaucrats and entrepreneurs seems to leave out the people of Hope Church whose 25 members worship in traditional ways, using an "outdated" liturgy and singing old hymns. What does Norris find to celebrate in the worship of Hope? How do you respond to her view of Hope?

5. Norris quotes an Episcopal priest and Rosebud Sioux, Martin Broken Leg: "Ghosts don't exist in some cultures," he said, adding dismissively, "They think time exists" (Reader, 132). How does Norris respond to the critique of contemporary American culture implied in this comment? What do you think of it?

8

Andre Dubus

The fictive universe of Andre Dubus is set in the region northeast of Boston where he himself has lived for the last several decades. It is a landscape of faded mill towns, small colleges, an accessible coastline, and a big city on the horizon. This is not to say that other personal worlds are absent from his work: there is the Cajun South where he was raised and the Marine Corps in which he served. But the literary soil most fertile for him has been the hardscrabble of New England, a working-class version of John Updike's more upscale Boston suburbia. His characters often live on the lower edge of the middle class: they keep house, own ice cream stores, work as cashiers and waitresses, and teach literature in order to try to write fiction. They marry early and divorce with pain; their children are their anchors.

When asked once to estimate the importance of religion to his work as a writer, Andre Dubus replied, "I see the whole world as a Catholic." On the one hand, this has meant curiosity about characters who have no faith, whose godless world the author must struggle to imagine precisely because their secularity is so foreign to him; on the other, it has meant attending to the spirituality of people like himself, raised in a Roman Catholic tradition and trying to understand the church's teaching in the midst of complex human experience. In either case, Dubus says, "I think my Catholicism has increased my sense of fascination and my compassion."[1]

What particularly compels his attention and elicits his compassion, moreover, is the urgency of moral choice, the necessity of making decisions and then of living with the consequences. For Dubus, moral life is the condition of all human existence, whether or not a character rises to the occasion or chooses to sidestep it, whether good and evil are recognized for themselves or only seen as a jam from which to escape. In his fiction there is always a conscience to confront.

Dubus is perhaps most eloquent when he writes specifically about Catholics, practicing or lapsed, for whom "almost anything is an ethical problem."[2] Often the arena of the problematic has to do with sexuality. His characters struggle over whether to have sex or not, to practice birth control or go to Mass, to maintain a vow of celibacy or respect the inviolability of marriage vows, to break one set of rules in order to obey another. From essays and interviews, it is clear that Dubus shares the opinion of Judy in the story "If They Knew Yvonne": "I don't think that the Church is so smart about sex."[3]

Nonetheless, whatever may be the author's disagreements with official teaching on artificial contraception or "self abuse," he is Catholic to his core in considering sexual matters to be of great importance. If the church has sinned in making people guilty, even fearful, about sex, it at least has not wrought the wholesale trivialization of sexuality that is one of the dubious gifts of the "sexual revolution." Our bodies are not simply flesh, but spirit too.

In his fiction, Dubus will often articulate his theology of the flesh through the words of clergy he no doubt wishes were actually in charge of the church. One thinks of Father Grassi in "If They Knew Yvonne," who hears the confession of a boy who no longer believes sex to be a sin and then assigns him as a penance to "say alleluia three times."[4] Or one thinks of Joe Ritchie in "Adultery," the fallen-away priest dying of cancer, who understands that the communion routinely celebrated at the altar is connected, at least in principle, to the one celebrated in bed: "Although he knew it was rarely true, he maintained and was committed to the belief that making love could parallel and even merge with the impetus and completion of the Eucharist."[5] The startling infusion of allegedly profane reality with the profoundly spiritual is one of the hallmarks of what Tobias Wolff has called Dubus's "unapologetically sacramental vision of life."[6]

If the love between a man and a woman only occasionally affords this insight, it is the love between a parent and a child that far more regularly takes characters beyond their own mortal boundaries and into the transcendent. Divorce makes this parental bond especially intense, as divided families and complicated custody arrangements heighten relationships that might otherwise be lost in the shuffle of ordinary life. Dubus writes out of his own experience in this regard, as he has revealed so movingly in his collection of personal essays, *Broken Vessels,* as well as portrayed in masterful stories such as "The Winter Father" or in the novella "Voices From the Moon." But it is "A Father's Story" that perhaps shows him at his most humanly poignant, as well as at his most theological, in his plumbing of the mystery of parental love.

The story has its origins in the author's interest in exploring the morality of the hit-and-run accident. At the same time he also wanted to write about a man of faith, "so I thought why not have the man of faith be the father of the one who does the hit-and-run."[7] In the end he created the story's narrator, Luke Ripley, "a big gutted, grey-haired guy," who has been divorced by his wife, Gloria, separated from his children, and left to discover how to live a life on his own. He describes the routines of his solitude, the bare outlines of his daily existence. But what matters most to him is the "real life" not apparent to the casual observer and communicated only to the parish priest. This is the life of faith that leads him (with a detour around the pope and the Vatican) to dedicate each day to God "as a prayer of thanksgiving," to ride his horse to the little parish church for early morning Mass, and to find in the ritual of the Eucharist (no matter how often his mind may wander) a renewal of himself in the "ceremony of love." In many ways he has the scrupulous temperament of the old-fashioned Catholic: he is an observer of rules, someone who has "subordinated feeling to action, for surely that is the essence of love"—someone who works to keep his conscience clear.

The austere beauty of Luke Ripley's world is suddenly shattered when his youngest child, a daughter home with him for a summer visit, wakes him in the middle of the night: "I hit somebody. With the *car*." He then acts on instinct and against every better judgment, indeed, against the judgment he would have followed had he been wakened in the night by one of his sons rather than by his daughter: "I would have phoned the police and told them to meet us with an ambulance at the top of the hill." As a result, while a young man is dead and his family deprived of a sense of justice, the girl drives away free. It does not matter to Ripley that he now has one secret he is not willing to confess or that he has violated not only the law of the state but almost anyone's sense of right and wrong. In fact, he tells God that he would do it all again, for what was wakened in him was an allegiance deeper than any other tie or obligation. No Abraham willing to plunge the knife into Isaac, nor a Father looking in silence upon his Son at Calvary, he is, on the contrary, "the father of a girl."

The story ends with prayer as a two-way conversation between apparent equals, as Luke Ripley speaks his mind freely and God answers in kind. It is essentially a standoff between fathers, a game that Ripley "wins" only by playing according to God's own crazy rules:

> So, He says, you love her more than you love Me.
> I love her more than I love truth.
> Then you love in weakness, He says.
> As You love me, I say ... *(Reader, 159)*

Here feelings are no longer subordinated to actions. The "essence of love" is utterly redefined, the law broken in favor of an illicit grace.

It would be a mistake to confuse what Luke Ripley does with what the author thinks his character should have done, just as it would be absurd to take "A Father's Story" as the definitive Dubus position on the morality of hit-and-run. Dubus has spoken of the controversy generated by this story in his interview with Lori Ambacher: "I came across two faculty women at a reading once who were angry about 'A Father's Story' because the father in that story covered up for the daughter's hit-and-run. And I think they got a little more angry because I said, 'I wouldn't do that. And my daughters wouldn't ask me to. I made this up.'"[8] It is easier to see sin than virtue in the cover-up, even a failure of Ripley's values. In the end, however, Dubus leaves us with the sense of an ethical violation and then of something beyond that trespass—God's trump card of redemption, the reminder of a "love in weakness" that is not human, but divine.

Peter S. Hawkins

Notes

1. Patrick Samway, "An Interview with Andre Dubus [1986], originally published in America (November 15, 1987), and reprinted in Thomas E. Kennedy, *Andre Dubus: a Study of the Short Fiction* (Boston: Twayne Publishers, 1988), 126-127.

2. Samway, *Andre Dubus*, 126.

3. *Selected Stories of Andre Dubus* (New York: Vintage Books, 1989), 193.

4. *Selected Stories of Andre Dubus*, 196.

5. *Selected Stories of Andre Dubus*, 445.

6. Tobias Wolff, introduction to *Broken Vessels*, by Andre Dubus (Boston: David R. Godine, 1991), xv.

7. Lori Ambacher, "A Conversation with Andre Dubus," *Image: A Journal of the Arts & Religion*, no. 3 (Spring 1993): 49.

8. *Image: A Journal of the Arts & Religion*, no. 3: 49-50.

A Father's Story

My name is Luke Ripley, and here is what I call my life: I own a stable of thirty horses, and I have young people who teach riding, and we board some horses too. This is in northeastern Massachusetts. I have a barn with an indoor ring, and outside I've got two fenced-in rings and a pasture that ends at a woods with trails. I call it my life because it looks like it is, and people I know call it that, but it's a life I can get away from when I hunt and fish, and some nights after dinner when I sit in the dark in the front room and listen to opera. The room faces the lawn and the road, a two-lane country road. When cars come around the curve northwest of the house, they light up the lawn for an instant, the leaves of the maple out by the road and the hemlock closer to the window. Then I'm alone again, or I'd appear to be if someone crept up to the house and looked through a window: a big-gutted grey-haired guy, drinking tea and smoking cigarettes, staring out at the dark woods across the road, listening to a grieving soprano.

My real life is the one nobody talks about anymore, except Father Paul LeBoeuf, another old buck. He has a decade on me: he's sixty-four, a big man, bald on top with grey at the sides; when he had hair, it was black. His face is ruddy, and he jokes about being a whiskey priest, though he's not. He gets outdoors as much as he can, goes for a long walk every morning, and hunts and fishes with me. But I can't get him on a horse anymore. Ten years ago I could badger him into a trail ride; I had to give him a western saddle, and he'd hold the pommel and bounce through the woods with me, and be sore for days. He's looking at seventy with eyes that are younger than many I've seen in people in their twenties. I do not remember ever feeling the way they seem to; but I was lucky, because even as a child I knew that life would try me, and I must be strong to endure, though in those early days I expected to be tortured and killed for my faith, like the saints I learned about in school.

Father Paul's family came down from Canada, and he grew up speaking more French than English, so he is different from the Irish priests who abound up here. I do not like to make general statements, or even to hold general beliefs, about people's blood, but the Irish do seem happiest when they're dealing with misfortune or guilt, either their own or somebody else's, and if you think you're not a victim of either one, you can count on certain Irish priests to try to change your mind. On Wednesday nights Father Paul comes to dinner. Often he comes on other nights too, and once, in the old days when we couldn't eat meat on Fridays, we bagged our first ducks of the season on a Friday, and as we drove home from the marsh, he said: For the purposes of Holy Mother Church, I believe a duck is more a creature of water than land, and is not rightly meat. Sometimes he teases me about never putting anything in his Sunday collection, which he would not know about if I hadn't told him years ago. I would like to believe I told him so we could have philosophical talk at dinner, but probably the truth is I suspected he knew, and I did not want him to think I so loved money that I would not even give his church a coin on Sunday. Certainly the ushers who pass the baskets know me as a miser.

I don't feel right about giving money for buildings, places. This starts with the Pope, and I cannot respect one of them till he sells his house and everything in it, and that church too, and uses the money to feed the poor. I have rarely, and maybe never, come across saintliness, but I feel certain it cannot exist in such a place. But I admit, also, that I know very little, and maybe the popes live on a different plane and are tried in ways I don't know about. Father Paul says his own church, St. John's, is hardly the Vatican. I like his church: it is made of wood, and has a simple altar and crucifix, and no padding on the kneelers. He does not have to lock its doors at night. Still it is a place. He could say Mass in my barn. I know this is stubborn, but I can find no mention by Christ of maintaining buildings, much less erecting them of stone or brick, and decorating them with pieces of metal and mineral and elements that people still fight over like barbarians. We had a Maltese woman taking riding lessons, she came over on the boat when she was ten, and once she told me how the nuns in Malta used to tell the little girls that if they wore jewelry, rings and bracelets and necklaces, in purgatory snakes would coil around their fingers and wrists and throats. I do not believe in frightening children or telling them lies, but if those nuns saved a few girls from devotion to things, maybe they were right. That Maltese woman laughed about it, but I noticed she wore only a watch, and that with a leather strap.

The money I give to the church goes in people's stomachs, and on their backs, down in New York City. I have no delusions about the worth of what I do, but I feel it's better to feed somebody than not. There's a priest in Times Square giving shelter to runaway kids, and some Franciscans who run a bread line; actually it's a morning line for coffee and a roll, and Father

Paul calls it the continental breakfast for winos and bag ladies. He is curious about how much I am sending, and I know why: he guesses I send a lot, he has said probably more than tithing, and he is right; he wants to know how much because he believes I'm generous and good, and he is wrong about that; he has never had much money and does not know how easy it is to write a check when you have everything you will ever need, and the figures are mere numbers, and represent no sacrifice at all. Being a real Catholic is too hard; if I were one, I would do with my house and barn what I want the Pope to do with his. So I do not want to impress Father Paul, and when he asks me how much, I say I can't let my left hand know what my right is doing.

He came on Wednesday nights when Gloria and I were married, and the kids were young; Gloria was a very good cook (I assume she still is, but it is difficult to think of her in the present), and I liked sitting at the table with a friend who was also a priest. I was proud of my handsome and healthy children. This was long ago, and they were all very young and cheerful and often funny, and the three boys took care of their baby sister, and did not bully or tease her. Of course they did sometimes, with that excited cruelty children are prone to, but not enough so that it was part of her days. On the Wednesday after Gloria left with the kids and a U-Haul trailer, I was sitting on the front steps, it was summer, and I was watching cars go by on the road, when Father Paul drove around the curve and into the driveway. I was ashamed to see him because he is a priest and my family was gone, but I was relieved too. I went to the car to greet him. He got out smiling, with a bottle of wine, and shook my hand, then pulled me to him, gave me a quick hug, and said: 'It's Wednesday, isn't it? Let's open some cans.'

With arms about each other we walked to the house, and it was good to know he was doing his work but coming as a friend too, and I thought what good work he had. I have no calling. It is for me to keep horses.

In that other life, anyway. In my real one I go to bed early and sleep well and wake at four forty-five, for an hour of silence. I never want to get out of bed then, and every morning I know I can sleep for another four hours, and still not fail at any of my duties. But I get up, so have come to believe my life can be seen in miniature in that struggle in the dark of morning. While making the bed and boiling water for coffee, I talk to God: I offer Him my day, every act of my body and spirit, my thoughts and moods, as a prayer of thanksgiving, and for Gloria and my children and my friends and two women I made love with after Gloria left. This morning offertory is a habit from my boyhood in a Catholic school; or then it was a habit, but as I kept it and grew older it became a ritual. Then I say the Lord's Prayer, trying not to recite it, and one morning it occurred to me that a prayer, whether recited or said with concentration, is always an act of faith.

I sit in the kitchen at the rear of the house and drink coffee and smoke and watch the sky growing light before sunrise, the trees of the woods near the barn taking shape, becoming single pines and elms and oaks and maples. Sometimes a rabbit comes out of the treeline, or is already sitting there, invisible till the light finds him. The birds are awake in the trees and feeding on the ground, and the little ones, the purple finches and titmice and chickadees, are at the feeder I rigged outside the kitchen window; it is too small for pigeons to get a purchase. I sit and give myself to coffee and tobacco, that get me brisk again, and I watch and listen. In the first year or so after I lost my family, I played the radio in the mornings. But I overcame that, and now I rarely play it at all. Once in the mail I received a questionnaire asking me to write down everything I watched on television during the week they had chosen. At the end of those seven days I wrote in *The Wizard of Oz* and returned it. That was in winter and was actually a busy week for my television, which normally sits out the cold months without once warming up. Had they sent the questionnaire during baseball season, they would have found me at my set. People at the stables talk about shows and performers I have never heard of, but I cannot get interested; when I am in the mood to watch television, I go to a movie or read a detective novel. There are always good detective novels to be found, and I like remembering them next morning with my coffee.

I also think of baseball and hunting and fishing, and of my children. It is not painful to think about them anymore, because even if we had lived together, they would be gone now, grown into their own lives, except Jennifer. I think of death too, not sadly, or with fear, though something like excitement does run through me, something more quickening than the coffee and tobacco. I suppose it is an intense interest, and an outright distrust: I never feel certain that I'll be here watching birds eating at tomorrow's daylight. Sometimes I try to think of other things, like the rabbit that is warm and breathing but not there till twilight. I feel on the brink of something about the life of the senses, but either am not equipped to go further or am not interested enough to concentrate. I have called all of this thinking, but it is not, because it is unintentional; what I'm really doing is feeling the day, in silence, and that is what Father Paul is doing too on his five-to-ten-mile walks.

When the hour ends I take an apple or carrot and I go to the stable and tack up a horse. We take good care of these horses, and no one rides them but students, instructors, and me, and nobody rides the horses we board unless an owner asks me to. The barn is dark and I turn on lights and take some deep breaths, smelling the hay and horses and their manure, both fresh and dried, a combined odor that you either like or you don't. I walk down the wide space of dirt between stalls, greeting the horses, joking with them about their quirks, and choose one for no reason at all other than the way it looks at me that morning. I get my old English saddle that has smoothed and darkened through the years, and go into the stall, talking to this beautiful creature who'll swerve out of a canter if a piece of paper blows in front of him, and if the barn catches fire and you manage to get him out he will, if he can get away from you, run back into the fire, to his stall. Like the smells that surround them, you either like them or you don't. I love them, so am spared having to try to explain why. I feed one the carrot or apple and tack up and lead him outside, where I mount, and we go down the driveway to the road and cross it and turn northwest and walk then trot then canter to St. John's.

A few cars are on the road, their drivers looking serious about going to work. It is always strange for me to see a woman dressed for work so early in the morning. You know how long it takes them, with the makeup and hair and clothes, and I think of them waking in the dark of winter or early light of other seasons, and dressing as they might for an evening's entertainment. Probably this strikes me because I grew up seeing my father put on those suits he never wore on weekends or his two weeks off, and so am accustomed to the men, but when I see these women I think something went wrong, to send all those dressed-up people out on the road when the dew hasn't dried yet. Maybe it's because I so dislike getting up early, but am also doing what I choose to do, while they have no choice. At heart I am lazy, yet I find such peace and delight in it that I believe it is a natural state, and in what looks like my laziest periods I am closest to my center. The ride to St. John's is fifteen minutes. The horses and I do it in all weather; the road is well plowed in winter, and there are only a few days a year when ice makes me drive the pickup. People always look at someone on horseback, and for a moment their faces change and many drivers and I wave to each other. Then at St. John's, Father Paul and five or six regulars and I celebrate the Mass.

Do not think of me as a spiritual man whose every thought during those twenty-five minutes is at one with the words of the Mass. Each morning I try, each morning I fail, and know that always I will be a creature who, looking at Father Paul and the altar, and uttering prayers, will be distracted by scrambled eggs, horses, the weather, and memories and daydreams that have nothing to do with the sacrament I am about to receive. I can receive, though: the Eucharist, and also, at Mass and at other times, moments and even minutes of contemplation. But I cannot achieve contemplation, as some can; and so, having to face and forgive my own failures, I have learned from them both the necessity and wonder of ritual. For ritual allows those who cannot will themselves out of the secular to perform the spiritual, as dancing allows the tongue-tied man a ceremony of love. And, while my mind dwells on breakfast, or Major or Duchess tethered under the church eave, there is, as I take the Host from Father Paul and place it on my tongue and return to the pew, a feeling that I am thankful I have not lost in the forty-eight years since my first Communion. At its center is excitement; spreading out from it is the peace of certainty. Or the certainty of peace. One night Father Paul and I talked about faith. It was long ago, and all I remember is him saying: Belief is believing in God; faith is believing that God believes in you. That is the excitement, and the peace; then the Mass is over, and I go into the sacristy and we have a cigarette and chat, the mystery ends, we are two men talking like any two men on a morning in America, about baseball, plane crashes, presidents, governors, murders, the sun, the clouds. Then I go to the horse and ride back to the life people see, the one in which I move and talk, and most days I enjoy it.

It is late summer now, the time between fishing and hunting, but a good time for baseball. It has been two weeks since Jennifer left, to drive home to Gloria's after her summer visit. She is the only one who still visits; the boys are married and have children, and sometimes fly up for a holiday, or I fly down or west to visit one of them. Jennifer is twenty, and I worry about her the way fathers worry about daughters but not sons. I want to know what she's up to, and at the same time I don't. She looks athletic, and she is: she swims and runs and of course rides. All my children do. When she comes for six weeks in summer, the house is loud with girls, friends of hers since childhood, and new ones. I am glad she kept the girl friends. They have been young company for me and, being with them, I have been able to gauge her growth between summers. On their riding days, I'd take them back to the house when their lessons were over and they had walked the horses and put them back in the stalls, and we'd have lemonade or Coke, and cookies if I had some, and talk until their parents came to drive them home. One year their breasts grew, so I wasn't startled when I saw Jennifer in July. Then they were driving cars to the stable, and beginning to look like young women, and I was passing out beer and ashtrays and they were talking about college.

When Jennifer was here in summer, they were at the house most days. I would say generally that as they got older they became quieter, and though I enjoyed both, I sometimes missed the giggles and shouts. The quiet voices, just low enough for me not to hear from wherever I was, rising and falling in proportion to my distance from them, frightened me. Not that I believed they were planning or recounting anything really wicked, but there was a female seriousness about them, and it was secretive, and of course I thought:

love, sex. But it was more than that: it was womanhood they were entering, the deep forest of it, and no matter how many women and men too are saying these days that there is little difference between us, the truth is that men find their way into that forest only on clearly marked trails, while women move about in it like birds. So hearing Jennifer and her friends talking so quietly, yet intensely, I wanted very much to have a wife.

But not as much as in the old days, when Gloria had left but her presence was still in the house as strongly as if she had only gone to visit her folks for a week. There were no clothes or cosmetics, but potted plants endured my neglectful care as long as they could, and slowly died; I did not kill them on purpose, to exorcise the house of her, but I could not remember to water them. For weeks, because I did not use it much, the house was as neat as she had kept it, though dust layered the order she had made. The kitchen went first: I got the dishes in and out of the dishwasher and wiped the top of the stove, but did not return cooking spoons and pot holders to their hooks on the wall, and soon the burners and oven were caked with spillings, the refrigerator had more space and was spotted with juices. The living room and my bedroom went next; I did not go into the children's rooms except on bad nights when I went from room to room and looked and touched and smelled, so they did not lose their order until a year later when the kids came for six weeks. It was three months before I ate the last of the food Gloria had cooked and frozen: I remember it was a beef stew, and very good. By then I had four cookbooks, and was boasting a bit, and talking about recipes with the women at the stables, and looking forward to cooking for Father Paul. But I never looked forward to cooking at night only for myself, though I made myself do it; on some nights I gave in to my daily temptation, and took a newspaper or detective novel to a restaurant. By the end of the second year, though, I had stopped turning on the radio as soon as I woke in the morning, and was able to be silent and alone in the evening too, and then I enjoyed my dinners.

It is not hard to live through a day, if you can live through a moment. What creates despair is the imagination, which pretends there is a future, and insists on predicting millions of moments, thousands of days, and so drains you that you cannot live the moment at hand. That is what Father Paul told me in those first two years, on some of the bad nights when I believed I could not bear what I had to: the most painful loss was my children, then the loss of Gloria, whom I still loved despite or maybe because of our long periods of sadness that rendered us helpless, so neither of us could break out of it to give a hand to the other. Twelve years later I believe ritual would have healed us more quickly than the repetitious talks we had, perhaps even kept us healed. Marriages have lost that, and I wish I had known then what I know now, and we had performed certain acts together every day, no matter how we felt, and perhaps then we could have subordinated feeling to action, for surely that is the essence of love. I know this from my distractions during Mass, and during everything else I do, so that my actions and feelings are seldom one. It does happen every day, but in proportion to everything else in a day, it is rare, like joy. The third most painful loss, which became second and sometimes first as months passed, was the knowledge that I could never marry again, and so dared not even keep company with a woman.

On some of the bad nights I was bitter about this with Father Paul, and I so pitied myself that I cried, or nearly did, speaking with damp eyes and breaking voice. I believe that celibacy is for him the same trial it is for me, not of the flesh, but the spirit: the heart longing to love. But the difference is he chose it, and did not wake one day to a life with thirty horses. In my anger I said I had done my service to love and chastity, and I told him of the actual physical and spiritual pain of practicing rhythm: nights of striking the mattress with a fist, two young animals lying side by side in heat, leaving the bed to pace, to smoke, to curse, and too passionate to question, for we were so angered and oppressed by our passion that we could see no further than our loins. So now I understand how people can be enslaved for generations before they throw down their tools or use them as weapons, the form of their slavery—the cotton fields, the shacks and puny cupboards and untended illnesses—absorbing their emotions and thoughts until finally they have little or none at all to direct with clarity and energy at the owners and legislators. And I told him of the trick of passion and its slaking: how during what we had to believe were safe periods, though all four children were conceived at those times, we were able with some coherence to question the tradition and reason and justice of the law against birth control, but not with enough conviction to soberly act against it, as though regular satisfaction in bed tempered our revolutionary as well as our erotic desires. Only when abstinence drove us hotly away from each other did we receive an urge so strong it lasted all the way to the drugstore and back; but always, after release, we threw away the remaining condoms; and after going through this a few times, we knew what would happen, and from then on we submitted to the calendar she so precisely marked on the bedroom wall. I told him that living two lives each month, one as celibates, one as lovers, made us tense and short-tempered, so we snapped at each other like dogs.

To have endured that, to have reached a time when we burned slowly and could gain from bed the comfort of lying down at night with one who loves you and whom you love, could for weeks on end go to bed tired and peacefully sleep after a kiss, a touch of the hands, and then to be thrown out of the marriage like a bundle from a moving freight car, was unjust, was intolerable, and I could not or would not muster the strength to endure it. But I did, a moment at a time, a day, a night, except twice, each time with a different woman and more than a year apart, and this was so long ago that I clearly see their faces in my memory, can hear the pitch of their voices, and the way they pronounced words, one with a Massachusetts accent, one midwestern, but I feel as though I only heard about them from someone else. Each rode at the stables and was with me for part of an evening; one was badly married, one divorced, so none of us was free. They did not understand this Catholic view, but they were understanding about my having it, and I remained friends with both of them until the married one left her husband and went to Boston, and the divorced one moved to Maine. After both those evenings, those good women, I went to Mass early while Father Paul was still in the confessional, and received his absolution. I did not tell him who I was, but of course he knew, though I never saw it in his eyes. Now my longing for a wife comes only once in a while, like a cold: on some late afternoons when I am alone in the barn, then I lock up and walk to the house, daydreaming, then suddenly look at it and see it empty, as though for the first time, and all at once I'm weary and feel I do not have the energy to broil meat, and I think of driving to a restaurant, then shake my head and go on to the house, the refrigerator, the oven; and some mornings when I wake in the dark and listen to the silence and run my hand over the cold sheet beside me; and some days in summer when Jennifer is here.

Gloria left first me, then the Church, and that was the end of religion for the children, though on visits they went to Sunday Mass with me, and still do, out of a respect for my life that they manage to keep free of patronage. Jennifer is an agnostic, though I doubt she would call herself that, any more than she would call herself any other name that implied she had made a decision, a choice, about existence, death, and God. In truth she tends to pantheism, a good sign, I think; but not wanting to be a father who tells his children what they ought to believe, I do not say to her that Catholicism includes pantheism, like onions in a stew. Besides, I have no missionary instincts and do not believe everyone should or even could live with the Catholic faith. It is Jennifer's womanhood that renders me awkward. And womanhood now is frank, not like when Gloria was twenty and there were symbols: high heels and cosmetics and dresses, a cigarette, a cocktail. I am glad that women are free now of false modesty and all its attention paid the flesh; but, still, it is difficult to see so much of your daughter, to hear her talk as only men and bawdy women used to, and most of all to see in her face the deep and unabashed sensuality of women, with no tricks of the eyes and mouth to hide the pleasure she feels at having a strong young body. I am certain, with the way things are now, that she has very happily not been a virgin for years. That does not bother me. What bothers me is my certainty about it, just from watching her walk across a room or light a cigarette or pour milk on cereal.

She told me all of it, waking me that night when I had gone to sleep listening to the wind in the trees and against the house, a wind so strong that I had to shut all but the lee windows, and still the house cooled; told it to me in such detail and so clearly that now, when she has driven the car to Florida, I remember it all as though I had been a passenger in the front seat, or even at the wheel. It started with a movie, then beer and driving to the sea to look at the waves in the night and the wind, Jennifer and Betsy and Liz. They drank a beer on the beach and wanted to go in naked but were afraid they would drown in the high surf. They bought another six-pack at a grocery store in New Hampshire, and drove home. I can see it now, feel it: the three girls and the beer and the ride on country roads where pines curved in the wind and the big deciduous trees swayed and shook as if they might leap from the earth. They would have some windows partly open so they could feel the wind; Jennifer would be playing a cassette, the music stirring them, as it does the young, to memories of another time, other people and places in what is for them the past.

She took Betsy home, then Liz, and sang with her cassette as she left the town west of us and started home, a twenty-minute drive on the road that passes my house. They had each had four beers, but now there were twelve empty bottles in the bag on the floor at the passenger seat, and I keep focusing on their sound against each other when the car shifted speeds or changed directions. For I want to understand that one moment out of all her heart's time on earth, and whether her history had any bearing on it, or whether her heart was then isolated from all it had known, and the sound of those bottles urged it. She was just leaving the town, accelerating past a night club on the right, gaining speed to climb a long, gradual hill, then she went up it, singing, patting the beat on the steering wheel, the wind loud through her few inches of open window, blowing her hair as it did the high branches alongside the road, and she looked up at them and watched the top of the hill for someone drunk or heedless coming over it in part of her lane. She crested to an open black road, and there he was: a bulk, a blur, a thing running across her headlights, and she swerved left and her foot went for the brake and was stomping air above its pedal when she hit him, saw his legs and body in the air, flying out of her light, into the dark. Her brakes were screaming into the wind, bottles clinking in the fallen bag, and with the music and wind inside the car was his sound, already a memory but as real as an echo, that car-shuddering thump as though she had struck a tree. Her foot was back on the accelerator. Then she shifted gears and pushed it. She ejected the cassette and closed the window. She did not start to cry until she knocked on my bedroom door, then called: 'Dad?'

Her voice, her tears, broke through my dream and the wind I heard in my sleep, and I stepped into jeans and hurried to the door, thinking harm, rape, death. All were in her face, and I hugged her and pressed her cheek to my chest and smoothed her blown hair, then led her, weeping, to the kitchen and sat her at the table where still she could not speak, nor look at me; when she raised her face it fell forward again, as of its own weight, into her palms. I offered tea and she shook her head, so I offered beer twice, then she shook her head, so I offered whiskey and she nodded. I had some rye that Father Paul and I had not finished last hunting season, and I poured some over ice and set it in front of her and was putting away the ice but stopped and got another glass and poured one for myself too, and brought the ice and bottle to the table where she was trying to get one of her long menthols out of the pack, but her fingers jerked like severed snakes, and I took the pack and lit one for her and took one for myself. I watched her shudder with her first swallow of rye, and push hair back from her face, it is auburn and gleamed in the overhead light, and I remembered how beautiful she looked riding a sorrel; she was smoking fast, then the sobs in her throat stopped, and she looked at me and said it, the words coming out with smoke: 'I hit somebody. With the *car.*'

Then she was crying and I was on my feet, moving back and forth, looking down at her, asking *Who? Where? Where?* She was pointing at the wall over the stove, jabbing her fingers and cigarette at it, her other hand at her eyes, and twice in horror I actually looked at the wall. She finished the whiskey in a swallow and I stopped pacing and asking and poured another, and either the drink or the exhaustion of tears quieted her, even the dry sobs, and she told me; not as I tell it now, for that was later as again and again we relived it in the kitchen or living room, and, if in daylight, fled it on horseback out on the trails through the woods and, if at night, walked quietly around in the moonlit pasture, walked around and around it, sweating through our clothes. She told it in bursts, like she was a child again, running to me, injured from play. I put on boots and a shirt and left her with the bottle and her streaked face and a cigarette twitching between her fingers, pushed the door open against the wind, and eased it shut. The wind squinted and watered my eyes as I leaned into it and went to the pickup.

When I passed St. John's I looked at it, and Father Paul's little white rectory in the rear, and wanted to stop, wished I could as I could if he were simply a friend who sold hardware or something. I had forgotten my watch but I always know the time within minutes, even when a sound or dream or my bladder wakes me in the night. It was nearly two; we had been in the kitchen about twenty minutes; she had hit him around one-fifteen. Or her. The road was empty and I drove between blowing trees; caught for an instant in my lights, they seemed to be in panic. I smoked and let hope play its tricks on me: it was neither man nor woman but an animal, a goat or calf or deer on the road; it was a man who had jumped away in time, the collision of metal and body glancing not direct, and he had limped home to nurse bruises and cuts. Then I threw the cigarette and hope both out the window and prayed that he was alive, while beneath that prayer, a reserve deeper in my heart, another one stirred: that if he were dead, they would not get Jennifer.

From our direction, east and a bit south, the road to that hill and the night club beyond it and finally the town is, for its last four or five miles, straight through farming country. When I reached that stretch I slowed the truck and opened my window for the fierce air; on both sides were scattered farmhouses and barns and sometimes a silo, looking not like shelters but like unsheltered things the wind would flatten. Corn bent toward the road from a field on my right, and always something blew in front of me: paper, leaves, dried weeds, branches. I slowed approaching the hill, and went up it in second, staring through my open window at the ditch on the left side of the road, its weeds alive, whipping, a mad dance with the trees above them. I went over the hill and down and, opposite the club, turned right onto a side street of houses, and parked there, in the leaping shadows of trees. I walked back across the road to the club's parking lot, the wind behind me, lifting me as I strode, and I could not hear my boots on pavement. I walked up the hill, on the shoulder, watching the branches above me, hearing their leaves and the creaking trunks and the wind. Then I was at the top, looking down the road and at the farms and fields; the night was clear, and I could see a long way; clouds scudded past the half-moon and stars, blown out to sea.

I started down, watching the tall grass under the trees to my right, glancing into the dark of the ditch, listening for cars behind me; but as soon as I cleared one tree, its sound was gone, its flapping leaves and rattling branches far behind me, as though the greatest distance I had at my back was a matter of feet, while ahead of me I could see a barn two miles off. Then I saw her skid marks: short, and going left and downhill, into the other lane. I stood at the ditch, its weeds blowing; across it were trees and their moving shadows, like the clouds. I stepped onto its slope, and it took me sliding on my feet, then rump, to the bottom, where I sat still, my body gathered to itself, lest a part of me should touch him. But there was only tall grass, and I stood, my shoulders reaching the sides of the ditch, and I walked uphill, wishing for the flashlight in the pickup, walking slowly, and down in the ditch I could hear my feet in the grass and on the earth, and kicking cans and bottles. At the top of the hill I turned and went down, watching the ground above the ditch on my right, praying my prayer from the truck again, the first one, the one I would admit, that he was not dead, was in fact home, and began to hope again, memory telling me of lost pheasants and grouse I had shot, but they were small and the colors of their home, while a man was either there or not; and from that memory I left where I was and while walking in the ditch under the wind was in the deceit of imagination with Jennifer in the kitchen, telling her she had hit no one, or at least had not badly hurt anyone, when I realized he could be in the hospital now and I would have to think of a way to check there, something to say on the phone. I see now that, once hope returned, I should have been certain what it prepared me for: ahead of me, in high grass and the shadows of trees, I saw his shirt. Or that is all my mind would allow itself: a shirt, and I stood looking at it for the moments it took my mind to admit the arm and head and the dark length covered by pants. He lay face down, the arm I could see near his side, his head turned from me, on its cheek.

'Fella?' I said. I had meant to call, but it came out quiet and high, lost inches from my face in the wind. Then I said, 'Oh God,' and felt Him in the wind and the sky moving past the stars and moon and the fields around me, but only watching me as He might have watched Cain or Job, I did not know which, and I said it again, and wanted to sink to the earth and weep till I slept there in the weeds. I climbed, scrambling up the side of the ditch, pulling at clutched grass, gained the top on hands and knees, and went to him like that, panting, moving through the grass as high and higher than my face, crawling under that sky, making sounds too, like some animal, there being no words to let him know I was here with him now. He was long; that is the word that came to me, not tall. I kneeled beside him, my hands on my legs. His right arm was by his side, his left arm straight out from the shoul-der, but turned, so his palm was open to the tree above us. His left cheek was clean-shaven, his eye closed, and there was no blood. I leaned forward to look at his open mouth and saw the blood on it, going down into the grass. I straightened and looked ahead at the wind blowing past me through grass and trees to a distant light, and I stared at the light, imagining someone awake out there, wanting someone to be, a gathering of old friends, or some-one alone listening to music or painting a picture, then I figured it was a night light at a farmyard whose house I couldn't see. *Going*, I thought. *Still going*. I leaned over again and looked at dripping blood.

So I had to touch his wrist, a thick one with a watch and expansion band that I pushed up his arm, thinking *he's left-handed*, my three fingers pressing his wrist, and all I felt was my tough fingertips on that smooth underside flesh and small bones, then relief, then certainty. But against my will, or only because of it, I still don't know, I touched his neck, ran my fingers down it as if petting, then pressed, and my hand sprang back as from fire. I lowered it again, held it there until it felt that faint beating that I could not believe. There was too much wind. Nothing could make a sound in it. A pulse could not be felt in it, nor could mere fingers in that wind feel the absolute silence of a dead man's artery. I was making sounds again; I grabbed his left arm and his waist, and pulled him toward me, and that side of him rose, turned, and I lowered him to his back, his face tilted up toward the tree that was groaning, the tree and I the only sounds in the wind. Turning my face from his, looking down the length of him at his sneakers, I placed my ear on his heart, and heard not that but something else, and I clamped a hand over my exposed ear, heard something liquid and alive, like when you pump a well and after a few strokes you hear air and water moving in the pipe, and I knew I must raise his legs and cover him and run to a phone, while still I listened to his chest, thinking *raise with what? cover with what?* and amid the liquid sound I heard the heart, then lost it, and pressed my ear against bone, but his chest was quiet, and I did not know when the liquid had stopped, and do not know now when I heard air, a faint rush of it, and whether under my ear or at his mouth or whether I heard it at all. I straightened and looked at the light, dim and yellow. Then I touched his throat, looking him full in the face. He was blond and young. He could have been sleeping in the shade of a tree, but for the smear of blood from his mouth to his hair, and the night sky, and the weeds blowing against his head, and the leaves shaking in the dark above us.

I stood. Then I kneeled again and prayed for his soul to join in peace and joy all the dead and living; and, doing so, confronted my first sin against him, not stopping for Father Paul, who could have given him the last rites, and immediately then my second one, or I saw then, my first, not calling an ambulance to meet me there, and I stood and turned into the wind, slid down the ditch and crawled out of it, and went up the hill and down it, across the road to the street of houses whose people I had left behind forever, so that I moved with stealth in the shadows to my truck.

When I came around the bend near my house, I saw the kitchen light at the rear. She sat as I had left her, the ashtray filled, and I looked at the bottle, felt her eyes on me, felt what she was seeing too: the dirt from my crawling. She had not drunk much of the rye. I poured some in my glass, with the water from melted ice, and sat down and swallowed some and looked at her and swallowed some more, and said: 'He's dead.'

She rubbed her eyes with the heels of her hands, rubbed the cheeks under them, but she was dry now.

'He was probably dead when he hit the ground. I mean, that's probably what killed—'

'Where was he?'

'Across the ditch, under a tree.'

'Was he—did you see his face?'

'No. Not really. I just felt. For life, pulse. I'm going out to the car.'

'What for? Oh.'

I finished the rye, and pushed back the chair, then she was standing too.

'I'll go with you.'

'There's no need.'

'I'll go.'

I took a flashlight from a drawer and pushed open the door and held it while she went out. We turned our faces from the wind. It was like on the hill, when I was walking, and the wind closed the distance behind me: after three or four steps I felt there was no house back there. She took my hand, as I was reaching for hers. In the garage we let go, and squeezed between the pickup and her little car, to tne front of it, where we had more room, and we stepped back from the grill and I shone the light on the fender, the smashed headlight turned into it, the concave chrome staring to the right, at the garage wall.

'We ought to get the bottles,' I said.

She moved between the garage and the car, on the passenger side, and had room to open the door and lift the bag. I reached out, and she gave me the bag and backed up and shut the door and came around the car. We sidled to the doorway, and she put her arm around my waist and I hugged her shoulders.

'I thought you'd call the police,' she said.

We crossed the yard, faces bowed from the wind, her hair blowing away from her neck, and in the kitchen I put the bag of bottles in the garbage basket. She was working at the table: capping the rye and putting it away, filling the ice tray, washing the glasses, emptying the ashtray, sponging the table.

'Try to sleep now,' I said.

She nodded at the sponge circling under her hand, gathering ashes. Then she dropped it in the sink and, looking me full in the face, as I had never seen her look, as perhaps she never had, being for so long a daughter on visits (or so it seemed to me and still does: that until then our eyes had never seriously met), she crossed to me from the sink and kissed my lips, then held me so tightly I lost balance, and would have stumbled forward had she not held me so hard.

• • •

I sat in the living room, the house darkened, and watched the maple and the hemlock. When I believed she was asleep I put on *La Boheme*, and kept it at the same volume as the wind so it would not wake her. Then I listened to *Madame Butterfly*, and in the third act had to rise quickly to lower the sound: the wind was gone. I looked at the still maple near the window, and thought of the wind leaving farms and towns and the coast, going out over the sea to die on the waves. I smoked and gazed out the window. The sky was darker, and at daybreak the rain came. I listened to *Tosca*, and at six-fifteen went to the kitchen where Jennifer's purse lay on the table, a leather shoulder purse crammed with the things of an adult woman, things she had begun accumulating only a few years back, and I nearly wept, thinking of what sandy foundations they were: driver's license, credit card, disposable lighter, cigarettes, checkbook, ballpoint pen, cash, cosmetics, comb, brush, Kleenex, these the rite of passage from childhood, and I took one of them—her keys—and went out, remembering a jacket and hat when the rain struck me, but I kept going to the car, and squeezed and lowered myself into it, pulled the seat belt over my shoulder and fastened it and backed out, turning in the drive, going forward into the road, toward St. John's and Father Paul.

Cars were on the road, the workers, and I did not worry about any of them noticing the fender and light. Only a horse distracted them from what they drove to. In front of St. John's is a parking lot; at its far side, past the church and at the edge of the lawn, is an old pine, taller than the steeple now. I shifted to third, left the road, and, aiming the right headlight at the tree, accelerated past the white blur of church, into the black trunk growing bigger till it was all I could see, then I rocked in that resonant thump she had heard, had felt, and when I turned off the ignition it was still in my ears, my blood, and I saw the boy flying in the wind. I lowered my forehead to the wheel. Father Paul opened the door, his face white in the rain.

'I'm all right.'

'What happened?'

'I don't know. I fainted.'

I got out and went around to the front of the car, looked at the smashed light, the crumpled and torn fender.

'Come to the house and lie down.'

'I'm all right.'

'When was your last physical?'

'I'm due for one. Let's get out of this rain.'

'You'd better lie down.'

'No. I want to receive.'

That was the time to say I want to confess, but I have not and will not. Though I could now, for Jennifer is in Florida, and weeks have passed, and perhaps now Father Paul would not feel that he must tell me to go to the police. And, for that very reason, to confess now would be unfair. It is a world of secrets, and now I have one from my best, in truth my only, friend. I have one from Jennifer too, but that is the nature of fatherhood.

Most of that day it rained, so it was only in early evening, when the sky cleared, with a setting sun, that two little boys, leaving their confinement for some play before dinner, found him. Jennifer and I got that on the local news, which we listened to every hour, meeting at the radio, standing with cigarettes, until the one at eight o'clock; when she stopped crying, we went out and walked on the wet grass, around the pasture, the last of sunlight still in the air and trees. His name was Patrick Mitchell, he was nineteen years old, was employed by CETA, lived at home with his parents and brother and sister. The paper next day said he had been at a friend's house and was walking home, and I thought of that light I had seen, then knew it was not for him; he lived on one of the streets behind the club. The paper did not say then, or in the next few days, anything to make Jennifer think he was alive while she was with me in the kitchen. Nor do I know if we—I—could have saved him.

In keeping her secret from her friends, Jennifer had to perform so often, as I did with Father Paul and at the stables, that I believe the acting, which took more of her than our daylight trail rides and our night walks in the pasture, was her healing. Her friends teased me about wrecking her car. When I carried her luggage out to the car on that last morning, we spoke only of the weather for her trip—the day was clear, with a dry cool breeze—and hugged and kissed, and I stood watching as she started the car and turned it around. But then she shifted to neutral and put on the parking brake and unclasped the belt, looking at me all the while, then she was coming to me, as she had that night in the kitchen, and I opened my arms.

I have said I talk with God in the mornings, as I start my day, and sometimes as I sit with coffee, looking at the birds, and the woods. Of course He has never spoken to me, but that is not something I require. Nor does He need to. I know Him, as I know the part of myself that knows Him, that felt Him watching from the wind and the night as I kneeled over the dying boy. Lately I have taken to arguing with Him, as I can't with Father Paul, who, when he hears my monthly confession, has not heard and will not hear anything of failure to do all that one can to save an anonymous life, of injustice to a family in their grief, of deepening their pain at the chance and mystery of death by giving them nothing—no one—to hate. With Father Paul I feel lonely about this, but not with God. When I received the Eucharist while Jennifer's car sat twice-damaged, so redeemed, in the rain, I felt neither loneliness nor shame, but as though He were watching me, even from my tongue, intestines, blood, as I have watched my sons at times in their young lives when I was able to judge but without anger, and so keep silent while they, in the agony of their youth, decided how they must act; or found reasons, after their actions, for what they had done. Their reasons were never as good or as bad as their actions, but they needed to find them, to believe they were living by them, instead of the awful solitude of the heart.

I do not feel the peace I once did: not with God, nor the earth, or anyone on it. I have begun to prefer this state, to remember with fondness the other one as a period of peace I neither earned nor deserved. Now in the mornings while I watch purple finches driving larger titmice from the feeder, I say to Him: I would do it again. For when she knocked on my door, then called me, she woke what had flowed dormant in my blood since her birth, so that what rose from the bed was not a stable owner or a Catholic or any other Luke Ripley I had lived with for a long time, but the father of a girl.

And He says: I am a Father too.

Yes, I say, as You are a Son Whom this morning I will receive; unless You kill me on the way to church, then I trust You will receive me. And as a Son You made Your plea.

Yes, He says, but I would not lift the cup.

True, and I don't want You to lift it from me either. And if one of my sons had come to me that night, I would have phoned the police and told them to meet us with an ambulance at the top of the hill.

Why? Do you love them less?

I tell Him no, it is not that I love them less, but that I could bear the pain of watching and knowing my sons' pain, could bear it with pride as they took the whip and nails. But You never had a daughter and, if You had, You could not have borne her passion.

So, He says, you love her more than you love Me.

I love her more than I love truth.

Then you love in weakness, He says.

As You love me, I say, and I go with an apple or carrot out to the barn.

Guides to Reflection

1. Luke Ripley first describes himself objectively, as he might be seen from the outside, as "a big-gutted, grey-haired guy, drinking tea and smoking cigarettes, staring out at the woods across the road, listening to a grieving soprano" *(Reader, 142)*. He then goes on to confess his "real life" as he experiences it on the inside—a life shaped by a Catholic upbringing, which begins each day with a "struggle in the dark of morning" *(Reader, 144)* and a dedication of the day to God. Talk about Luke's character, looked at externally and from within. What kind of "man of faith" has Dubus succeeded in creating?

2. During a conversation about faith, Father Paul tells Luke Ripley that "Belief is believing in God; faith is believing that God believes in you" *(Reader, 147)*. What do these definitions mean to you? Are they useful in thinking about "A Father's Story"?

3. What is the distinction between Luke Ripley's love for his sons and that which he feels for his daughter? Discuss his assertion to God: "I could bear the pain of watching and knowing my sons' pain, could bear it with pride as they took the whip and nails. But You never had a daughter and, if You had, You could not have borne her passion" *(Reader, 159)*.

4. After Luke Ripley discovers the corpse of the young man his daughter has killed inadvertently, he feels God present everywhere in the scene, "in the wind and the sky moving past the stars and moon and fields around me, but only watching me as He might have watched Cain or Job" *(Reader, 154)*. How do these biblical characters enrich our understanding of the way Ripley feels?

5. When Dubus was criticized by other writers for allowing Luke Ripley other choices than those he himself would make in a comparable situation, he replied: "My approach to art is to become someone else in a situation which I construct and to try through imagination and gifts and other mysteries to go into the human heart. It's a mistake that what's on the page has anything at all to do with what the writer would do in that situation."[1] How do you react to this reply?

Notes

1. Lori Ambacher, "A Conversation with Andre Dubus," *Image: A Journal of the Arts & Religion*, no. 3 (Spring 1993), 49-50.